Haunted by Mary Queen of Scots

The author has had the good fortune to meet
Mary Queen of Scots on several occasions
and this book tells that fascinating story.

by

Neil Burns

2001

Published by JocknDoris Publishers

ISBN No 0 9535748 1 4

Printed in England by
The Amadeus Press, Cleckheaton
Typesetting by
Highlight Type Bureau Ltd, Bradford
Photographs by
John Pitt, Abberley, Worcs.

For

JocknDoris Publishers
P O Box 112, Kidderminster
Worcs DY11 7SS

www.jockndoris.co.uk

Dedications
Dot and Carry-one and the four kittens who have been friends of mine all
along - Pretty, Biscuit, Houdini and Panic - all characters in their own right.

PROLOGUE

Why write this book?

Having published my first book at the insistence of two amazing ladies called Lily Cove and Mary Queen of Scots, I have now asked myself why both of those wonderful women kept appearing to me - always asking for me to do something for them.

In the instance of Lily Cove, she led me down a path so clearly defined that I was able under her directions to solve the mystery of her apparent death in 1906 from a parachuting accident. In fact she didn't die then, as you will have read in my book called "A few special Ghosts I have met".

On the back cover of that book I wrote "the author admits to being in love with Mary Queen of Scots" and whilst that is even more true now, I did not understand why it was so, then.

Whilst my memory for short term events is becoming increasing poor like many people of increasing years, my memory of long ago events appears to be getting sharper and when I read an amazing book by Dr Brian Weiss called 'Many Lives, Many Masters', I became increasingly aware that possibly those memories could be tapped.

Dr Weiss is a Florida psychiatrist who tells a true story of one of his patients who had several unfortunate problems which he was having great difficulty in curing, until he decided to try hypnosis to see if his patient had had experiences in her youth which were causing her problems.

He was very surprised when under hypnosis for the first time, his patient started to describe herself in totally unfamiliar surroundings which turned out to be in ancient Egypt. She described her work as an embalmer using oils and essences and when awake after the session she had no knowledge of what these oils were used for and in fact did not even know where to find Egypt on the map.

This appeared to be a memory from a "Past Life" and there are many thousands of examples of "Past Lives" which can be proved quite easily. Children have described to their parents in great detail, villages in France where they know they could never have been. Yet when they get there, for the very first time, they can show their parents where the church is, where the village green and shop are, and then of course round this corner is where we all used to live.

I was encouraged to go to a Hypnotherapist to see if I had any memories of "Past Lives" of my own. I found a wonderful lady called Paula Hollaway in Bewdley, Worcs., who over a series of weeks put me into a simple hypnotic trance for an hour every Saturday morning.

These were not only a relaxing pleasure but an amazing revelation to me. Each session consisted of a opening chat where we discussed the previous week's events and solved most of the worlds problems between us! Then I would lie on the couch and be put very easily into a trance, when after a few minutes I would see a beautiful all encompassing blue colour and drift off into a Wonderland.

Paula tells me that during the sessions, I speak very slowly and with some difficulty and sometimes poor grammar and she compiles notes of what I have said as we progress. Afterwards I am very sleepy and tired, but the following day my memory of the events come pouring out and I am able to write creatively from these long ago memories.

I recall in detail about a life I had as thirteen year old school boy in Germany in the 1930's and also much further back as a young mathematician in the Inca period.

But the recurring theme goes back always to the time of Mary Queen of Scots where I appear to be completely at home. My first recollection was as a young page boy, one of who's duties was to bring dry logs to Mary Queen of Scots to keep her fire blazing and keep her Majesty warm. When I failed to do so she scolded and punished me in a way I will never forget calling me all the time "young Anthony".

Now history tells that Mary was given, by her Captor the Earl of Shrewsbury, a pageboy who was called Anthony Babington, when she was held at Sheffield Castle and Sheffield Manor.

I have become more and more convinced that in a past life I was young Anthony Babington, who later of course was to play a pivotal role in the so called Babington plot, which eventually gave Elizabeth the excuse she needed to have Mary executed.

This whole question of "Past Lives" begs the question of reincarnation. If we have been on this earth before as someone else, then surely we can reasonably expect to return again later. That means we get a fresh start - a new chance to live another life. Many people say your performance in the current life dictates

4

the conditions in your next life, so that if you have been miserable, unreasonable and unkind in this life, so you can reasonably expect to be on the receiving end of those traits in your next life.

Possibly if you have worked extraordinarily hard this time round, then you will be given a much cushier lot in the next, and so forth.

If we believe in reincarnation, it makes life a whole lot more bearable, and there is the not inconsiderable advantage of being immortal, so the fear of death disappears. There is also the great thought that you will be able to see again, those people that you loved and cared for in this life, who have already left us.

The book tells of my search for Mary Queen of Scots, and my past life as her page boy Anthony Babington. I have been fortunate enough to meet her regularly as a Ghost and have been able to help her in many ways. But the final chapter of her story has still to be written.

My Meetings with Mary Queen of Scots

I have a very special relationship with Mary Queen of Scots as you will soon learn as you read this book, and I have always known that I have some very special things still to do for her. I now know that one of those is to re-open the Spa at Buxton where she had at least four happy sojourns in the 1570's.

This story will go both back in time to recall where and how I have met and helped Mary Queen of Scots and forward in time to tell you how I plan to repay her kindness. Only the benefit of hindsight at a much later year will convince any reader that I am correct.

Many books have been written about that beautiful but tragic Queen who had on her tombstone etched by her son, "Queen of Scotland by birth, Queen of France by marriage and Queen of England by expectation".

She became Queen of Scotland when her father died in 1542 when she was only six days old. She was sent to France for safety in 1547 and wooed both the French King and his Court and later married his son the Dauphin of France. She became Queen of France when her father-in-law died to leave young Francis the new young King of France.

Many argue still that Mary had a better right to the Throne of England than Elizabeth who kept her captive for 19 years and never had the courage to meet her face to face. Suffice it to say that it was Mary's son James, who became the first joint King of Scotland and England, and all the crowned heads of Europe are descended directly from Mary, and not from the spinster Queen.

I have now seen Mary on twelve occasions. I have written about them in chronological order as far as Mary's age is concerned. All of these are drawn from my recollection of the events exactly as I recall them. Whether they come from a "Present Life" or one of my "Past Lives", or even a "Future Life", I leave to the reader to decide.

INDEX

Mary Queen of Scots
A very brief history

For those of you not familiar with the History of Mary Queen of Scots I have noted some of the high points below. Please bear in mind that I am trying to condense into two pages what Antonia Fraser covered in eight hundred , and of course as "I admit to being in love with Mary Queen of Scots", I must be just a little bit biased.

She was born in Linlithgow Palace in central Scotland in 1542 and when she was only six days old, her father, the King of Scotland, died.

And so, not yet a week old, she became Mary Queen of Scots.

From that day on it seemed that men and women fought over her and almost always for their own ends. At the age of five she was sent to France for safety and lived in the Champagne country, looked after by her mother, Mary of Guise. Mary was an immediate hit at the French Court.
When she was barely old enough, she married Francis, the Dauphin of France in an arranged wedding designed to cement friendly relations between Scotland and France. Mary was always very fond of him and they spent many happy times together but Francis was unfortunately a sickly child and was prone to suffer from all known ailments. He was destined to become King of France earlier than expected, when his father, Henry II, was tragically killed in a jousting contest, with his successful opponent becoming the most unpopular man in France for accidentally killing his own King. So at only sixteen years old, Mary became Queen of France as well as Queen of Scotland. Her husband the king was a chronic invalid and unfortunately died after only two years on the throne, so Mary became a widow at eighteen.

At this time there was turmoil in Scotland, with infighting between the clansmen all vying to get rid of the Consort who ruled on her behalf.
Mary returned by sea and landed at Leith, the port of Edinburgh wearing all her French finery having just come from the finest court in Europe. She was met by an oxcart to carry her through the dank, wet streets of Edinburgh to the Castle at the top of the Royal Mile. It was extremely cold and she must have been miserable as none of her subjects recognised their Queen who had, remember, been their Queen for nearly two decades already.

Mary and her few friends slowly imposed themselves on the unruly Scots Lords and, over two or three years, a reasonable court was established. She married Lord Darnley also of royal blood and sent specially by her cousin Queen Elizabeth. Although he was tall and dashing and it started well, Darnley was a very weak man who drank too much, and let Mary down on many occasions. He did however father Mary's only son who later became James VIth of Scotland and James Ist of England so uniting the two countries. Through him every subsequent monarch including the present Queen is descended directly from Mary Queen of Scots.

A plot was hatched to use gunpowder to blow up a house called Kirk'o Field where Darnley was staying. The plot was bungled because although the House was blown to smithereens, Darnley escaped injury only to be strangled in his nightgown in the garden outside. It remains an unsolved mystery who actually killed Darnley. Lord Bothwell was one of the few men audacious enough to mount such a plan, but as it failed he can hardly be guilty of any crime. In any event Darnley was already dying of Syphilis. Unfortunately everybody jumped to the wrong conclusion and although Mary supported and later married Bothwell, it proved to be a very unpopular and unfortunate marriage.

She survived many battles fought over her. She was captured and imprisoned on a number of occasions one of the best remembered sojourns being on an island in Loch Leven, where she escaped after her food servant smuggled her a key under her napkin.

Of course, Mary had an undeniable right to the throne of England. Henry the Eighth had six wives and many argue, especially Catholics like Mary, that divorce was not legal and all his children by every Queen after the first one, were illegitimate.   This made Elizabeth illegitimate in their eyes, and Mary her full cousin was next in line through her grandfather Henry VIIth and therefore, the rightful Queen of England.

Queen Elizabeth was acutely aware of this and feared that Mary would rally Catholic support for her cause which could easily have swept her to power. Mary decided on impulse to go to England and try and get help from her cousin but Elizabeth's men captured her and she was imprisoned in many Castles and Manor Houses for nineteen long years. In fact she spent more of her life in England than in either Scotland or France.

At first she was well looked after by the Earl of Shrewsbury and the incomparable Bess of Hardwick staying at Buxton, Chatsworth, Sheffield, and Wingfield amongst others.

Many plots were hatched to rescue her and put her on the throne of England. Some say the Spanish raised the Armada specially to rescue her but it came too late. Elizabeth's Spymaster Walsingham who intercepted her secret messages eventually tricked Mary and the so-called Babington Plot was uncovered. In a mock of a trial she was found guilty and later beheaded at Fotheringhay.

Alloa Tower (Mary Aged 3 years)
A little girl at Alloa Tower

I attended the Marie Stuart Society Annual General Meeting at Newbattle Abbey, Dalkeith on 15th April 2000.

This marvellous occasion was the seventh Annual General Meeting of the Society who's sole object is the study and furtherance of Mary Queen of Scots. The meeting in the morning went very smoothly as it always does under the Chairmanship of Margaret Lumsdaine.

Lunch was served downstairs in the vaulted dining room and afterwards the Duke of Hamilton was invited to become the Patron of the Society. As the premier Earl in Scotland it was a great honour for the Society to have him. In his short acceptance speech he was both witty and modest.

Then Margaret Lumsdaine our President introduced the Earl of Mar who was to give the main address of the day. He started in relatively witty style with repartee with the Duke of Hamilton about his ancestor being the only Regent of Scotland in Mary's day not to be executed by the Hamiltons!

Then followed an hour of the History of the Erskine family who although they were the family responsible for bringing up the royal children in Stirling Castle, and the Earl was the keeper of the Keys, there was nothing at all about Mary which disappointed the gathering. He did mention however the extensive restoration of Alloa Tower with its very strong door and two hundred year old lock which was still in use.

I slept for part of it and was bored and a bit disillusioned. In hindsight this was a Classic situation developing for me. I went and cleared the room in Newbattle Abbey where I was staying and paid the janitor and packed the car ready to leave.

I offered lifts to the German girl Claire and Archie Macpherson a retired Scots Solicitor but neither accepted. As I left however, I saw a lady walking down the drive. She turned out to be the one who recited the verses in English in Mary's honour earlier and I gave her a lift to Waverley Station.

Then I meandered towards the Forth Road Bridge a little grumpy at having to pay the double fare for going one way only! I then phoned my mother expecting her to be delighted that I would be visiting her in a couple of hours.

I spoke to my bother-in-law David who was there at her house. There seemed no urgency to get there so I thought just to finish off the day, I would go to Alloa Tower which had recently been renovated by the speaker the Earl of Mar.

I arrived at 5.40pm and no one was there, as the doors had been locked some ten minutes earlier.

I walked round and round the foot of the big vertical square tower which is imposing and yet desolate at the same time. I saw the imposing front doors with the rounded arch of intricate ironwork at the top. I also saw the heavy handle and with keyholes at top and bottom which Lord Mar had commented on in his speech earlier in the day. These had apparently been used for over two hundred years.

The third time round I realised that I had been thinking of Mary as fully grown but of course she had been just a little toddler when she was a visitor here when brought for a few days from her main home at Stirling Castle.

As I came round the corner in the biting wind there was a little toddler of a girl in a cap and long dress shivering outside the front door. Her sleeves seemed only to come to her elbows as if she had slightly outgrown the dress.

"Please let me go in because I am cold, very cold" she said and I obliged by opening the door by the old central handle and let the little girl slip in to the warmth inside. I closed the door and started walking back to the car where two policemen were giving a ticking off to a local young motorist.

I went inside the quadrangle of small houses close by to see if anyone was there but all was very quiet.
I caught the policemen as they were setting off. They were amazed at my story and confirmed the time as 5.50pm and came and checked the door was locked, and as I had no key, it would have been quite impossible for me to have opened the door.

I gave them a copy of the book and told them to watch out for any lost little toddlers and if they found any to give me a call. I set off for Drymen and stopped off for a bite to eat after seeing a big sign to Macdonald's in Stirling.

I had a little fun in their unusual queuing system and as I sat afterwards in the car park, what I thought was a policeman rushed in with a toddler in a cap, and I was feeling very pleased with myself as my prediction had come true!!

However when the man came out with the toddler and his meal, I asked him if he was a policeman. He laughed and said "No - I am a Prison Officer !!"

On the way to Drymen I telephoned Margaret and Ian to tell them the story and they gave me Lord Mar's telephone number to ring the following morning.   I caught him just as he having breakfast and he suggested I ring his Manager Peter de Sallis who would be opening up later in the day.

He seemed very excited by my story and I suggested to him that he should look very closely for anything unusual inside the Tower as usually when Mary appears she is trying to give me a message of some kind.

Imagine my delight when I heard that a little tiny pair of woollen knitted gloves had been found just inside the door. Maybe this was another way of Mary saying to me "Please keep me warm!"

* * * * *

In trying to build up a picture of Mary, the only clues I got from this meeting were that she was going to be tall, elegant and composed, if a little gangly and she had a clear voice and a cheeky smile as she swept inside the door.

Rheims Cathedral
The young Queen of France

As I recalled in chapter 25 of "A few special Ghosts I have met", I met Mary as a young seventeen year old girl when I was in Rheims Cathedral in France.

In 1988, I went with a coach party of office colleagues to France, to the Champagne country near Rheims to the North East of Paris.

It was a very happy party and it was my good luck to sit next door to a stunning young girl called Helen, who had joined the party at the very last moment because of a cancellation.

We set off from Kidderminster at two in the afternoon, and as we were a party of wine lovers setting off on holiday to see and taste many interesting French wines, it was not surprising that the first cork was heard to pop just as the wheels of the coach started to roll.

We were in high spirits throughout the journey and eventually arrived for an evening meal at a hotel in the outskirts of Reims, where we straggled in to be booked in at the reception.

As Helen was rather tired, I picked her up and carried her in, rather like a husband traditionally carries his wife over the threshold, and this caused great amusement to about fifty German tourists who were, I think, on a similar trip to our own.

When later our party of thirty went down to our enormous table, the Germans started singing their wedding song and, much as Helen and I protested that we were not getting married, in fact we weren't even yet good friends, nothing would shake the Germans from their belief.

As the evening progressed, Helen and I took the line of least resistance, saying "If you can't beat them, join them," and we thoroughly enjoyed playing the part.

As I got some help from the rest of the party, a great cheer went up from the Germans as we carried Helen into her room onto her bed and she was fast asleep by the time we shut the door.

After breakfast, I went for a short walk to buy the usual postcards and was intrigued to see one referring to Mary of Guise, who apparently had lived here. She was, as you all know, the mother of Mary Queen of Scots and I asked someone if they knew about Mary.

All I could discover was that she was known as Marie Stuart and someone said that there was Champagne named after her.

Later in the day we had three or four visits to the vineyards, and the cellars of the various Champagne houses. They were all excellent in their way, with the best, as you might expect, at the magnificent head office of Moet et Chandon, the biggest of them all.

As we were leaving, Helen called me to one side and said she had lost her purse. It must have been left at one of the previous cellars. All the others, of course, wanted to continue with the trip, so I volunteered to take Helen back to find her purse, saying to her as we went that I had something else to find.
The concierge found us a taxi and we explained to the driver in my best French where we needed to go. The driver like everyone in France, assumed we were eloping or certainly heading for a frisky afternoon somewhere, but we persuaded him to take us back the way we had comer, and fortunately we recovered the purse the second stop.
We had agreed to meet the rest of the party at Reims Cathedral later that afternoon but we had time to explore, and I took Helen in search of Marie Stuart.

We asked the driver whether he knew anything about Mary Queen of Scots and although I am sure I described Mary's marriage to Phillip the Dauphin of France, it was only when I said Marie Stuart that he exclaimed "Rue Marie Stuart!!". He knew a street called Marie Stuart.

We set off to find it and this seemed to trigger his memory as he told us of "le tragedie" of the "petite jeune Reine de France" - the small, young queen of France. We arrived at Rue Marie Stuart and as I could see the Cathedral towering above the city, within easy walking distance, I paid off the taxi driver and Helen and I walked up a street a little off the beaten track.

We saw a plaque on the wall saying Champagne de Marie Stuart and we realised we had stumbled on to the headquarters of the company selling this champagne.
I rang the bell and asked nicely if we could enquire about the Champagne de Marie Stuart, and got a reception which was, to say the least, frosty. I think we would have stayed on the doorstep forever trying to inveigle our way in, had I not said "but the champagne is for the Mademoiselle ici" - for Helen standing beside me.

The director of the Company was summonsed, and as soon as he arrived, immediately showed extraordinary deference to my young companion, seeming almost to recognise Helen. We were ushered in and given the Royal treatment, with first call always to Helen.
I then saw a magnificent life size portrait of Mary Queen of Scots, called, of course, Marie Stuart and as I turned towards Helen, it was obvious that they had

all noticed the uncanny likeness of Helen to that portrait.

Did they think this was Mary returned to visit them?

Did they maybe think that Helen was a descendant of Mary's? They clearly held her in considerable awe.

Helen was oblivious to all the attention, saying only to me, "They seem awfully nice people here!"

I asked about Mary and whether she lived here and they, of course replied that she was part of the House of Guise. She eventually married the Dauphin of France when she was sixteen until his tragic death two years later when she was eighteen. Helen was also eighteen years old.

We tasted the specially poured champagne and were given a complimentary bottle, and we warmly thanked the Director, who gave his very special card to Helen, You must come and visit us anytime, Mademoiselle."

We then set off for the Cathedral and walked what turned out to be quite a long way through the streets, till all of a sudden we were outside it and asked a lady selling leaflets "can we go in?"

"Of course but please speak to Madame Pompadour inside the main door", she replied.

As she was saying this she excitedly tugged her own companion's arm and pointed towards Helen, who again just walked casually beside me. The companion set off at a run for the cathedral and hurled inside in undue haste.

I started to feel intense excitement as we walked towards the massive doors of the Cathedral, which were (of course) closed, as are the main doors of most Cathedrals.

To my amazement, they started to open as Helen and I walked towards them.

I think I was invisible. All eyes were on Helen and as she walked in I could hardly breathe for excitement, as the people all around us looked on in awe of Helen. This must surely be Marie Stuart returned to visit them.

Helen and I walked round as tourists might, and I asked questions of them about Marie Stuart, and they all looked in puzzlement as if to say "surely you already know her well?"

We went to the front of the massive altar and I stood, exhilarated, with enormous happiness and a swelling in my chest as if something wonderful was happening - it was almost mystical- even magical and although Helen was interested and enjoying it, I could sense that she felt no special excitement at all.

We walked back towards the main door, and thanked Madame for telling us about the Cathedral and she wished Mademoiselle well, with instructions to me

"look after her well when you take her back to Scotland."
I had not previously mentioned Scotland, and as I have no discernible accent, so this surprised me, but Helen said, "she always was a bit of a nag, Madame, always telling me to look after myself".

As we swept out into the square we saw the rest of the party approaching and rushed over and were quickly engulfed by them.
I wanted to go back and was disappointed to see the doors were now shut. There was a queue, albeit a short one, at the little entrance at the side of the main doors.
As I went in, it felt cold, and Madame who had spent nearly half an hour with Helen and me didn't seem to recognise me. I asked her if she would open the doors, because it would be marvellous.
"Oh no Monsieur", she said, "the doors never open - the last time they were opened was when Marie Stuart left for Scotland".

"Let me see the doors", I said, and I went to the base of the doors and the massive hinges were encrusted with rust and had not moved in many decades.
Madame looked me straight in the eye and said, "You see, Monsieur, you must be mistaken. The doors of Reims Cathedral have been closed since 1561"
As I returned to the party, there was Helen telling the others how wonderful it was in the Cathedral, and how you could see everything - it was so light and airy inside.

* * * * *

This episode confirms that Mary was charming with a warm smile, tall, elegant - stunning is the word that comes to mind, and was already used to people gazing at her and she did not seem phased by it at all. She knew she was beautiful and that seemed to make everyone happy. Remember she was already Queen of France and had brought Paris to a halt when she was married in the open air outside Notre Dame Cathedral the previous year.

Linlithgow Palace
Searching for a balcony

As I recalled in Chapter 24 of my book I saw Mary at Linlithgow Palace when she came to the balcony above the chapel and thanked me for finding the way to it for her.

I was returning to my brother's house near the tiny village of Kilconquhar, in Fife, one afternoon when I had a sudden urge to make a detour to Linlithgow Palace, which I had never seen but which is reputed to be haunted by Mary Queen of Scots.

I had the afternoon free so I headed off towards Linlithgow, which is not far from Edinburgh but nevertheless a little off the beaten track.

I found the town quite easily but struggled to find the Palace as I went past it two or three times before someone showed me the very narrow road which led to it.

I arrived at maybe four o'clock in the afternoon and was surprised that there was only one other car in the parking area.

I went in and found a rather fat lady in the little shop saying "You can buy a ticket for three pounds but it's not haunted you know", which I felt was a fine example of salesmanship.

Well I was as disappointed as she expected me to be, with only a ruin of a building with no furnishings at all and whilst I dutifully went up to the top of each tower, I saw and felt nothing.

I did however meet a party of three Americans who were rather noisily taking pictures of each other rather than Linlithgow Palace.

I made some remark about their making so much noise that it was no wonder the ghost did not appear, and I told them that I had come to see the ghost of Mary Queen of Scots, who is supposed to haunt the Palace.

"I know that she used to stay here and, in particular, used to worship in a little Chapel within the Palace", I told them. They were intrigued but unconvinced.

After a lot of struggle, seemingly going round and round without finding it, I eventually went though an inner door and there was the chapel.

Just four walls now and a very high roof but there was a strange gallery set in to one wall, which was higher than one story, but not as high as two, if you understand me.

There was a railing so that you could stand there and look down into the chapel and I had an urge to go up there.

It must be connected I thought and, being very careful to retrace my steps, I went in search of the missing link to get there.

Now these Palaces had many circular staircases and unless you have a built in compass, you very soon lose the sense of direction; "where is north?" I simply couldn't tell and to make matters worse, the exits from these circular staircases do not all come out at the same angle or in fact on the same floor.

I tried and tried to find the way to that gallery and eventually, because I was getting tired, I went to the shop at the bottom and said, "Please could you help me find the way to the gallery overlooking the chapel".

"That is very easy", she replied, "follow me!" And I started off after her but as I did so, as so often happens, I started to limp because when I am tired the one leg is a lot better than the other.

This slowed the fat lady down and, although we walked a long way, we couldn't find it and she was amazed. "You stay here and I will find it and come back for you, although why you are going to all this fuss is beyond me".

Well she came back in maybe five minutes saying, "I can't find it. You will just have to leave." I said, "that is ridiculous - you will have to give me my money back!" That made her take notice and she said "I will call my husband" and off she went. Her husband was just as confident of finding it - which should have been simplicity itself, especially as he knew every nook and cranny of the Palace.

He returned after a few minutes and said, "I give up", and just as I was getting cross and about to demand my money back, the three Americans arrived saying "we have seen a gallery above the chapel but we had a terrible job finding our way out."

"Show me the way", I said and they took me straight to the gallery, to find the fat lady and her husband standing below us in the chapel, looking very pleased with themselves. "We knew you would find it eventually," said the fat lady. "Remember you must leave by six o'clock!".

I was thanking the Americans and pointing out to them that you could see through the tall windows, which had no longer any glass in them, towards the main gate and we were all admiring the symmetry of the architecture when the tall figure of a lady appeared inside the gate.

I first spotted her and then touched the arm of the American lady who whispered, "Be quiet, Luke, there is someone coming!"

We saw through the same window the main gates being closed, as our lady walked straight for us towards the natural door, but unfortunately she went out of our sight, blocked by the wall of the chapel.

I began to feel very funny and looked at Luke, who was as pale as a sheet. "You can't leave now, Luke," said I, as over his shoulder I saw the most beautiful and radiant lady approach through the archway on to our gallery.

She came and stood between Luke and me and looked demurely down into the Chapel. She was tall and graceful, beautifully dressed in a bodice waistcoat and long dark skirt, all of which were richly embroidered. Her face was serene and beautiful and I recognised her immediately.

She said "I am very grateful to you for finding this precious place for me. I have looked for many years but no one has ever matched my determination to find it." She stood in silence, oblivious to our presence as her eyes searched the floor of the chapel inch by inch.

"I am satisfied now", she said, "thank you again kind sir!" and she swept past us towards that archway and was gone.

Luke was now white and his wife much the same as I said "You realise that was Mary Queen of Scots and I think we have done her a great service". Poor soul, she has been looking for this spot for over four hundred years and I got frustrated after less than an hour!"
The little boy with them said, "who was that nice lady? - There she goes again!" and we all saw Mary striding happily towards the main gate.
"Oh there you are!" shouted the fat lady's husband - "we have been looking everywhere for you. The main gate was shut at six o'clock and we want to go home."
"You mean that no one has been after six o'clock", I asked
"That's right and it is now six thirty", said she with feeling.
"How did that lady get out then?" said the little boy and his parents grabbed him and headed to the archway and downstairs.

I was still tired and my hip hurt but I followed the sounds of the Americans and in a relatively short time was in the shop.
"Thank goodness", said the man "we thought we had lost you forever".
"You didn't sell a ticket to a beautiful young lady, did you?", I checked.
"We did not!", replied the fat lady, "we are not allowed to sell after six o clock and anyway the doors were locked!"
"Mary Queen of Scots has been here so many times she doesn't need a ticket now", I said "Keep an eye out for her in the gallery - she knows how to get there now".
The next day in the papers an article described how three Americans had seen Mary Queen of Scots at Linlithgow Palace, although for some strange reason they didn't mention me!

* * * * *

Mary was confident and tall, a lady in her prime at twenty one years old but concerned about the privacy of her worship which was very important to her. She was worried that people could overlook her. She gave us all a warm smile when she said "Thank you" which made me blush to the roots.

Stirling Castle
Audience with a Queen

As I recalled in Chapter 26 of my book, I visited Mary in her chambers at the very top of Stirling Castle going through the beautiful gardens which magically exist there.

Imagination is a powerful force and I have become able to transport myself purely by imagination to the most faraway places and times - if you believe it - you are there.

I lived during the seventies in a wonderful little village called Saline in Fife where, you will recall I met Sir Walter Scott, and Saline in turn was close to Stirling which used to be the main stronghold of Scotland, and some say, the real capital.

I had had also lived in Edinburgh and knew it well, so when I woke up one morning in 1567 I found myself in familiar surroundings near Linkfield House, just across the road from Musselburgh golf links, one of the first places where the game was ever played.

I was wearing shorts and had lots of wavy hair, so I guessed I was maybe eighteen or so, and as I walked back towards Edinburgh a group of horsemen were riding the same way at a leisurely pace.

"Young man!" shouted one of them, "we need good strong young chaps like you, follow us", and I saw no reason not to follow this bold looking man, who later I learned later was James Hepburn, Earl of Bothwell, the man destined to marry Mary Queen of Scots. I immediately took to him as he had an air of leadership and a charisma that set him above the others.

There was a cart amongst the party, drawn by an old horse and I leapt aboard leaving behind me Musselburgh, which I grew to know very well later when I was at school there.

I was getting used to seeing places many years removed from when I knew them but I also understood that my knowledge of later year's events could help the people currently here, not that I would give them any unfair advantage, merely give them the benefit of my knowledge.

"Where are you going" I asked "To see our Queen, of course" they cried, and I was overjoyed! " Where will she be?" I asked, "she has called us all to Dunfermline Abbey in Fife, where she has gathered a meeting, but we are not sure how to get there. Which way should we go?". Without thinking I said " We must cross at Queensferry."

I knew that the Firth of Forth almost cut Scotland in half and although Dunfermline was just across the water, the only way to get there other than by ferry, was the very long trek via Kincardine Bridge which could take two to three days.
We wound through the country lanes until we came to the ferry at Queensferry, where I had crossed many times to go to school, thus knew it well. It is the point where Fife and the Lothians come closest and a natural spot for a ferry. This saved us at least two days of travel- all the way past Linlithgow and back over the bridge at Kincardine - but I wasn't aware of that at the time.

It took all day to cross, because the ferry was only big enough for 50 men and we were 200 strong. So we rested and slept until the following morning when we set off for Dunfermline, which was where my father was born some 345 years later.

I didn't feel strange at all because at every point I knew something which was of value to the party. I remembered for instance the Haws Inn at South Queensferry, where I had a wonderful dinner once with Archie Stewart and Minta and we made many important decisions about John Menzies at that hotel.

It is hidden for good reason and I managed to smuggle the Earl of Bothwell there when he expressed the need for food and a little wine. Bothwell told me that he was certain we could not have reached Dunfermline in time, had it not been for the ferry which I knew about and he said "Her Majesty will be pleased."
When we arrived at Dunfermline Abbey, Bothwell took me to him to meet Mary Queen of Scots, and I was overwhelmed because Mary remembered me and greeted me with warmth. I, of course, had met her at Linlithgow and helped her then, but for her to remember, was wonderful.

"Young sir - you look well!" said Mary. "And I, your Majesty am delighted to see you again", I replied. "Please may I be of service to you?". "Of course you may; what would you wish me to do?" she enquired.

"Please do not travel south to England without Bothwell to guard you, because Elizabeth means to capture you and imprison you", I said.

"Stay here, I implore you, and I will ask the Lords to rally behind you till you are strong. By that time I, too, will be strong enough to go with you and Bothwell with an army to guard you. We will gather support in England from all good Catholics and you will eventually be Queen of England, as is your right!"

"I know I have to give you this message and I fear you will not heed it, but please listen to someone who knows what will happen." "Tell me more at Stirling " she was all she said.

Stirling Castle commands the whole centre of Scotland dominating the central plain which stretches almost from coast to coast, and it must have been a daunting sight for any opposing army.

The highest point around for many miles, the Castle was built on a huge outcrop of rock and the building came to the very extremity on three sheer sides. The fourth side looks out onto the joining of two rivers, another marvellous natural defence.

The walls were a continuation of the rock, so any person planning to scale then would be exhausted before they got very far.

Inside the castle there is a palace and a huge chapel, and right at the very top the royal apartments. As if in complete contrast to the rest of the Castle, in one corner there is a fabulous garden sheltered from the winds by the walls, and this was the haven where Mary chose to live. Safe, you would have thought from all danger, and having the beauty of nature to enjoy in her favourite garden full of wild plants and bushes of all descriptions.

Historians have it that Bothwell and his retinue did not make it in time to Dunfermline. In their absence the other Lords persuaded Mary to go to England to make peace with Elizabeth, and we all know that she was captured, imprisoned for 19 years and then beheaded.

If only Mary had taken my advice then.

Loch Leven
Long beautiful hair

I used to travel regularly from Saline in the West of Fife to St Andrews or Elie on the East Coast and every journey you would skirt Loch Leven. To go to the north was a better road but slightly longer, to the south was the scenic route close to the mountainside where they do a great deal of hang-gliding. but which ever way you chose it was beautiful, if a little slow.

Quite unlike Loch Lomond where the road travels for many miles at Water Level, both the roads are set at about 100 feet above the water level and so you have a commanding view of all that you can survey. There is an outpost of the Royal Bird Observatory where people come from all over the world to watch the wild bird life.

Just like Loch Lomond, however, Loch Leven has many islands set in its waters, some tiny, some a little bigger and the biggest is where they set Loch Leven Castle. Sitting starkly on a green island stands the castle built many centuries ago and the only way to get there is by boat, too far to swim, far too far to swim as some who tried to rescue Mary Queen of Scots found to their cost. It fact you have to know the route very well to get there safely by boat as there are rocks, shallows, other little islands, not to mention the Loch Leven trout to circumvent.

Mary was imprisoned there by her own people in 1567 when she lost a vital battle of confrontation near Dunbar and she was handed over to the Douglas family for safekeeping. She stayed at Loch Leven Castle for almost a year and most historians say it was a miserable year but I don't think so.

I went there one Sunday and like many others had a monumental struggle to find the ferry. When you find it, is very efficiently run indeed. Every twenty minutes or so a little boat run by the Highlands and Islands Board sets off from a little jetty and then takes a highly circuitous route through the shallows to wind its way to the other jetty at the other end beneath the castle walls.

As I was putting on my heaviest overcoat as it was bitterly cold, two cars drew up beside me amid screams of delight as the bevy of children and adults struggled out of the cars. All the children were partially disabled and this clearly was a fun day out for them.

I offered the leader of the group my help but she declined saying politely that they all like to make their own way, some are a little slower than the others. There was also a collie dog with its leg in a bandage and as we set off for the jetty we must have looked a motley crew, but the boat driver took it in his stride and we struggled a board.

I was surprised that there was no ticket to purchase, until I realised that when you got there you were a captive market. If you chose not to pay, then I think your stay might have been as long as that of Mary Queen of Scots had been.

We arrived at the jetty and I saw the children all ashore and then headed off for the Ticket Office. I wrote in the book there "Visit to see Mary Queen of Scots" and I asked if it was haunted and the big man behind the desk laughed saying "good lord no!"

So the mood was very light hearted as I went to explore the Castle which is very well preserved. There is a main Tower which is three stories high and you can access all flights with protected balconies for visitors. I was approached there by a middle-aged lady who very nicely asked "what are you doing here?" in an American accent. "Looking for Mary Queen of Scots", was my simple and honest reply. "So am I", she said, "but I have had no luck so far."

"And neither you will!" said a tall Scot "as she won't be found here".
As the rest of my party rather loudly arrived at the foot of the stairs I thought it would be much quieter outside, so I went for a walk on the top of the castle walls with 360 degree panoramic views, confirming that there was no escape without a good boat and someone to row it expertly through the shallows.

Directly opposite the Main Tower is the Glassen Tower which is only two stories high and contains only one room on each floor. I had really given up any chance or hope of seeing Mary as I went to a position halfway up the stairway, where you could look across to the other side of the room. In the far wall there were several oval shaped holes which I presume had been used to throw out all manner of things, many years ago. I was looking rather lazily at one at head height, when I realised that if you let your focus go, you could see way through the hole to the trees beyond. I was trying to focus on the leaves and get a bearing of exactly where we were, when the oval shape turned into a series of diamond shapes and then through the oval came a figure who settled on a chair beside the wall.

She was elegant, serene and confident, and very tall, and there was not the slightest doubt that this was Mary Queen Of Scots. She had long beautiful hair which she was brushing in long languorous strokes like a person stroking a favourite cat or dog and she was enjoying what she was doing.

She was too far away to speak to, but she was so clearly content, elegantly dressed and looking so well that I got the message loud and clear, that she had been happy at Loch Leven not thoroughly miserable as most historians claim.

Almost without me noticing I had been joined by the Scots couple who stood on either side of me, and I whispered to the girl " She has beautiful hair don't you think?" and she said, "yes she does but who is she?" and her husband asked "who are you both talking about?"

"Do you not see a lovely lady figure sitting across there combing her hair?" and he said "no I do not", and I said "well if you will only relax and let me show you how it is done" and I explained how he must look at the oval and let it drift away till it turned to diamonds and he sighed and said "of course, how beautiful she is!"

We were all gazing in awe at Mary when I spotted my American friend who snuggled up beside us and she said "what are you all looking at?", and I moved a pace back and she moved in ahead of me and without any instructions she saw straight away what we were experiencing.

"I knew we would see her today" , she said "how wonderful!", and we just drank in the happy sight until some other tourists came barging in with cameras and she was gone.

I had the message though and had seen my lovely Mary again and I walked back to the Ticket office to tell the man there what I had seen and pointed out to him what I written in the visitors book. "Can I add to it please?", and I wrote that we had seen the wonderful Mary with long beautiful hair.

Apparently he now shows people how to do it and of course only a few can, but isn't it marvellous that her memory is permanently there and it is a happy memory?

It was such a happy place and I wanted to stay but I saw my disabled friends boarding the ferry and I rushed to join them. "Have you had a good time?" I asked and they all beamed back at me - one offering me the remains of her chocolate bar which is just about the nicest thing she could possibly have done! What a wonderful day.

* * * * *

What a wonderful disposition Mary must have had, to be cheerful and smiling through captivity and her warmth clearly spilled over the children.   It also confirmed that until she cut her hair, whilst escaping near Dumfries, she had fabulous long tresses of a very dark auburn colour, which shone when she brushed them in front of us.

Castle Bolton
Third floor prisoner

I can recall vividly in dreams, the awesome sight of Castle Bolton in Yorkshire, which is constructed like a set of four towers, each square and straight up. I remember being trapped there night after night in this formidable fortress. Cold but comfortable it was, and frustrating too, because the Castle has some outstanding views and Mary must have been able to see for long distances, and yet was not free to travel even one mile.

I visited Castle Bolton with Judy the mother of the girl Katie who has the most beautiful legs in England and whose company makes beautiful cheese out of goats milk. I was given the name of the owner by Keith Cheetham the local Chairman of the Marie Stuart Society and all Keith would say was "ask for Harry, he will show you round."

When we arrived at the imposing building we walked up a long flight of steps to an outer door on the second floor. There I asked one of the staff casually, "Is Harry in today?", to which a very distinguished man strode forward saying "Do you mean me?".

I asked "Are you Harry?. I was told to ask for you by Keith Cheetham who I hope you remember", to which he replied, "of course I remember Keith he was here not so long ago".

"We would particularly like to see the rooms which were occupied by Mary Queen of Scots.", and he said "of course I can show you, please follow me." He was a perfect host, and when I asked him who owned the building, he merely said "it has been in my family since it was built in 1157". We were talking to the owner!!

We saw various rooms, which are still well preserved, all in the same tower section where Mary and her party of 51 were housed together with the very impressive Great Hall where she would greet visitors. We climbed right to the very top to the room where Mary slept and it had a much warmer, friendlier feel to it.

We saw the room which most people remember, with a model of Mary Queen of Scots and one of her handmaidens in attendance, but it was the room on the very top above, where I rested on the very bed she used on the top floor.

I felt at ease in this topmost room, and lay for some time on Mary's bed, which gave me a feeling exactly the same as I have in my own bed, when I drift away in the morning on one of my magical imaginary trips to Cape Town or Edinburgh Castle.

As I lay there I heard rustling on the staircase and two figures appeared. One was the tall elegant figure of Mary Queen of Scots and the other a much shorter one who I took to be Mary's secretary as they walked together to her desk, speaking what I took to be French.

Mary was wearing a beautiful heart-shaped cap made of white silk embroidered with pearls which covered her ears and on the outside, black silk reached down to her shoulders accentuating her lovely slender neck.

They spoke far too quickly for me to understand, but they were both agitated in that Mary clearly wanted a message or letter to be sent very quickly. How this would be done I was not sure, but the secretary was writing as quickly as he could on to a parchment. I know that all Mary's messages had to be put into code to avoid falling into the wrong hands and clearly this would take some time.

Both Mary and her secretary then took off their caps and reached in to find the cypher which they both used to put the message into code. It is the first time I had ever noticed her cap in detail but now I realised the two white heart-shaped areas were not only for show - they had a purpose of their own. Her hair was dark and cut short.

Eventually Mary finished dictating and bade farewell to the secretary who bowed and left retreating backwards as one always must.

To my amazement Mary turned towards me and said "you do not yet understand French, do you young Anthony?", and " I shall teach you to speak the language, because it is the most expressive and beautiful of all the languages I have learnt".

"May I take a message for your Majesty?" I asked.
"Are you returning to Scotland soon? " she enquired.
"Yes of course I am - to whom must I take the message?"
She said "You must find a tall man who plays golf at St Andrews and is well known to the people but lives over the seas so as not to pay taxes. Tell him that I want him to restore the monarchy to Scotland so that we can be strong again".
"There must be a parliament with good men and women drawn from all parts of Scotland to decide how we must rule the country". "Tell them that I approve, and will give them my blessing and just like my direct descendant Queen Elizabeth now addresses the Houses of Parliament, I too will come and address them in Edinburgh". "Like her, I may not agree with my ministers but they have

been appointed by the people and they must decide. If they ever wish to meet me, they must go to Nether Kinnedar", she decreed. This sent a shiver down my spine, because Nether Kinnedar is a house I know well, owned by good friends of mine in Saline in Fife.

With that I heard footsteps on the stairs, and heard Judy's voice say "I knew you wouldn't find anyone up here" and Mary just melted away.
I had my instructions and so it mattered not at all.

Judy and I thanked Harry warmly for his hospitality and set off to a point not far way called 'Mary's Scarf', where legend has it that Mary tried to escape from Bolton Castle, and when on horseback ran too close to a bramble bush, and her scarf was torn from her shoulders. This was later found by the following horsemen and, unfortunately, helped them track her down.

When Judy and I got there we sat at the spot and looked across the valley way way into the distance. Down below we could see there was a small cemetery and I immediately had the urge to investigate.
There we walked up and down the gravestones until I stopped at one and said to Judy, "Do you know a John Castleton" and she stopped abruptly and said "Yes I do - what an incredible thing - I often wondered where Mr Castleton was buried as there were some important questions I wanted to ask him as he was a real mentor to me before he tragically died."

"We have been led here," I said, "come and sit quietly on this seat and wait."
Judy looked rather puzzled but we walked across and sat down, one on either end of the long seat in the cemetery.
Judy was too tense and expectant, and I could not get her to relax, so I said, "don't worry - I am probably mistaken - nothing is likely to happen", and her shoulders sagged and she sort of gave up, and in a few minutes I could see her dozing.

I too was in a little bit of a trance having just seen Mary Queen of Scots, and didn't really notice this tall elegant man slide past and sit down between us.
I passed the time of day with him and he said he was hoping to see Judy, and I reached across and tapped Judy on the knee. She looked up and saw her mentor and without any hesitation they started talking.
I stepped politely backwards, and slipped away up to the top of the cemetery where there was another seat and resumed my nap.

What seemed like twenty minutes passed and there was Judy standing in front of me. "You knew he was there to see us, didn't you?" and I said, "did he answer all your questions?"   "Oh yes", was all she said.

Sheffield Manor
Over Her Majesty's knee

When I went to see where Mary Queen of Scots had been held in the Tower at Sheffield Manor, I met Jerry Boden the stonemason who showed me round the whole building, most of which unfortunately is a ruin.

The turret Tower is the only part of the building which remains inhabitable, and it is an austere Tower if ever there was one. Three stories high, straight up and down, with no softening frills of Architecture or design.

Each floor has two rooms interlinked with the very narrow winding staircase running up all three floors at the one corner. There is only one way to go and I was led by Jerry up to the top floor where, even I, was stunned by the starkness of it. We then went into Mary's room to see her effigy standing there in the corner.

It was only a fairly basic attempt at depicting her and unfortunately the model figure was not tall enough or slim enough to be the real Mary. The children who made it, had done well with the face though, which was true to the portraits I have seen, but of course she was inanimate and rather disinterested, standing in the corner.

There was an armchair by the huge fireplace, and as soon as Jerry had left me with her, I moved the Chair across to be more friendly. I gave her a present of a little bag of cinnamon to make mulled wine, and a copy of my book and the inevitable Mars bar, which is a welcome present at any time.

I sat with her for nearly three hours, in happy mood and became attracted to the shape and the colour of her beautiful mouth, which I could not resist lightly kissing. Although the alabaster was cold it gave me a real thrill to gently kiss her lips and her nose seemed to nuzzle mine and thought I saw a tremor or tremble go across her face as I withdrew.

I kissed her from the right and found I could reach her mouth with comfort and ease, but strangely I could not do so from the left which puzzled me. She then seduced me without lifting a finger or flickering an eyelash and I became aroused and hard which I have not done for several years in that manner.

I wasn't remotely tired or spent as you usually are. I sat in the armchair and relaxed completely and when I opened my eyes, the room was full of Mary's party. All were there except the Earl of Bothwell who was in a separate prison in Denmark. They were quiet and the four Mary's were all doing needlework alongside Mary Queen of Scots who was already nearly finished her famous canopy which stood behind her chair of State. I was fascinated by their clothes and the serenity they all had, considering that they had been in captivity for several years.

It was beautifully warm with a blazing fire with quite a few spare logs ready to go onto the fire. We closed the building and locked the door after saying a fond farewell to Mary, not kissing her of course because I don't think Jerry would have quite understood.   I had a uneventful journey back and awaited developments.

Later I floated back to see Mary Queen of Scots at Sheffield Manor, as I was worried about her being cold.   Today the heating there consists of a miserable radiator which is kept luke warm and really does not even take the chill off the temperature.   There is however a perfectly splendid fireplace, together with a chimney, which could easily be lit to give huge amounts of heat as required.

On going back I recall seeing Mary in her finest black dress standing in the corner, cold and miserable and regaling her little page boy Anthony Babington for being slow in getting logs for her fire.   The little lad was maybe thirteen or fourteen years old, and seemed only to be able to bring a few logs each time, up the winding staircase, three stories up to Mary's special room at the top. The logs were wet and when he put them on the fire, they merely caused it to go out rather than give any heat at all.

Anthony was distraught, but Mary was angry, and realised that Anthony must be taught a lesson otherwise they would all freeze to death.   Anthony worshipped his Queen, as all her party did, and he was only a boy and possibly had been distracted when out gathering wood, whereas his Queen was confined to the Tower unable, because of her rules of captivity, to go outside.

"Come here, Anthony Babington", she commanded "I must teach you a lesson you will never forget", and Anthony moved with trepidation across to his Queen's side.   Mary Queen of Scots sat down and smoothed her skirts and hauled young Anthony over her knee into the classic spanking position. She then gave him some considerable whacks with the palm of her hand.   Apart from some embarrassment this had no effect at all on young Anthony, so Mary ordered him to stand up and unbuckle his belt and drop his breeches to the floor. With fumbling fingers Anthony did so, revealing a fine pair of lily-white legs covered only on top with a pair of loose pants which gave little protection.

"I am going to smack your bottom until it is raw, young Anthony, so that you never let me run out of logs, good dry logs, ever again", said Mary Queen of Scots determined to exert her authority. With that she started to smack his poor little bottom with vigour and it turned from lily-white to a fairly bright red in no time at all. Anthony was bearing it well but his pride was hurt enormously at being spanked by his Queen, but he must stand the pain and only cried out a little. Mary cajoled him throughout, saying that he was lazy and had let Her Majesty down.

Anthony protested that he couldn't help it, and would do better in future promising to redouble his efforts. His bottom was turning scarlet when I noticed that instead of trying to avoid the blows, he was merely sinking into his Queen's lap more and more, and when she commanded him to stand up he did so with his little Willie very much to attention in front of him. This did not go unnoticed by his Queen, who turned him round and examined what was causing his pants to stick out at right angles. She tore down his pants and threw him over her lap again saying, "you are enjoying this, you rascal, and it is not a punishment at all!"

Anthony was now grinding himself into Mary's knee and she had two alternatives - one to carry on smacking Anthony's bottom in which case he was going to decorate her lovely gown with some very young sperm, or she would have to stop the punishment. "Stand up" she commanded "and let me see you." Anthony stood up in obvious agony/ecstasy not knowing what to do. As Mary turned him round towards her and attempted to put his Willie back where it belonged, her fingers just brushed against his Willie. This was just too much and he shot his little load onto the floor in a little pool right in front of Mary. His expression was a picture - in sheer heaven but acute embarrassment at the same time.

"Have you learnt you lesson young Anthony?" said Mary.

"Oh yes, your majesty, I will gather the logs vigorously for you from now on."

"I hope I never have to do that again" said Mary - not really meaning it, as it too had stimulated her, and Anthony said "Of course, I will do everything to make sure it never happens again, Your Majesty", but you could tell from his voice that he didn't mean a word of it.

As I looked at Anthony a shiver went through me as I realised for the first time that I was indeed seeing myself. I was young Anthony and had had my first experience of spanking at the hands of a Queen - a tall lovely Queen who had smacked my little bottom with her lovely hands and long delicate fingers. I would be smitten with spanking for the rest of my life.

Anthony gathered himself and his clothes together and sped from the room.

Later that afternoon he asked permission to put a few logs beneath the stairs inside the front door. He set up a buffer stock there which would always be dry - ready to light at any time and warm Her Majesty. From that day on the Queen was warm, and had a special affection for young Anthony Babington who kept his promise of never letting them run out of logs again.

He did however sometimes admit to his Queen of other misdemeanours he had inadvertently perpetrated, and the Queen quite rightly decided that only a spanking could solve or settle such a matter. So Anthony's bottom was warmed from time to time by a Queen who realised that it was an important part of his training as a pageboy.

As for the author it explains in one short chapter his enduring love of both spanking and tall women. Just writing it has caused his rather old and very tired little Willie to stir in memory.

When Anthony Babington grew into a man, he had to leave Mary and go his own way. He settled in a good house in London and was successful in business.

Walsingham, who was Queen Elizabeth's Spymaster, was always looking for ways to trap Mary Queen of Scots into an apparent plot to overthrow Queen Elizabeth and put Mary as Queen on the throne in her place. He got wind of the fact that Mary was constantly sending letters out to people across Europe asking for support. All of these were in code and when Walsingham intercepted these and cracked the code, it was easy for him to intercept Mary's messages and alter them. He was able to draw Babington into a plot, which only required Mary's support, for the King of Spain to invade and rescue Mary and put her on the throne.

Unfortunately not only did Babington fall for this, but vigorously recruited his friends to form a ring of conspirators, all of whom were of course known to Walsingham. When the time was right he took the letters to Queen Elizabeth, who ordered the conspirators arrested and put in the Tower. Mary Queen of Scots was put on trial for treason. In a mockery of a trial, where there was no chance of her receiving anything other than a guilty verdict, she was sentenced to be executed and was later beheaded at Fotheringhay Castle.

* * * * *

Could Babington have averted what happened? I don't think so. It was all orchestrated by Walsingham who was in complete control. On the basis that I was Babington, whatever could I have done about it?

Old Hall Hotel Buxton
A day to Buxton

I go twice a year to a splendid exhibition of lingerie and swimwear in Harrogate once in February and again in August, which is highly recommended to anyone who likes to see beautiful girls in the latest most exotic underwear. It certainly recharges my red corpuscles for another few months at least.

I sometimes meet my editor Alastair Burnet there and so I phoned him to say I was planning to be there on the Sunday. He however had already planned an important game of golf at Ganton, so couldn't make it but he said in passing that he had found the most wonderful place to stay at a town called Buxton. He had gone on a promotional visit and stayed at the Old Hall Hotel where apparently Mary Queen of Scots had stayed four hundred years ago. "Its famous for its natural Springs" said Alastair and of course I remembered where I had seen the name - on the supermarket shelves – where Buxton water is well known.

Well I needed no further bidding, and I phoned the hotel right away to see if I could stay on the way back from Harrogate. Unfortunately the room in which Mary stayed, called Mary's Bower, was not available till Thursday so I booked in there and then for that Thursday night.

The days dragged till Thursday but eventually it came, and I got all my affairs in the office tidy so I could sneak away early. Buxton is just over a hundred miles from Mamble, straight up the M5/M6 Motorway to Junction 17, and then across an amazingly twisty and turny road, up and down the Dales of Derbyshire, till you eventually arrive at a place which claims to be the highest town in England.

And what an amazing place it is - a total surprise as part of old England has been preserved. There are some truly beautiful buildings, including an ornate Opera House with lavish finishings not only inside but out. Plush velvet chairs and painted ceilings inside a building with any number of unnecessary towers and glass, all to make your enjoyment of the opera more complete.
Buxton has any number of really beautiful buildings, including one at the hospital which has the biggest unsupported slate dome in England. There is another huge domed hall where the Beatles are reputed to have performed, and a huge swimming bath complex for all to enjoy, just past the botanical gardens where quite free of charge you can meander in the warm atmosphere amongst tropical plants in their element.

It is a positive pleasure palace, very much enjoyed by the Victorians and during the early decades of the twentieth century, but sadly now almost unheard of since the nineteen seventies.

And it was all mine to enjoy.

I arrived at the hotel in a state of some excitement because going to see my wonderful Mary Queen of Scots is always a thrill. Room 26 is Mary's Bower with a huge four poster bed with its traditional awning with ornate frills round the edges supported by beautiful wooden pillars.

On the bed sat a welcoming drawer sachet, perfumed with Mary Queen of Scots herbs, which I opened immediately, to fill the room with a lovely fragrance both invitational and warm.

The room oozed of Mary, and portraits and drawings of her were all around.

When I last saw Mary at Wingfield Manor, I stood close to her under the huge old Walnut Tree there, which supposedly started from a walnut dropped by Anthony Babington when he disguised himself as a gypsy using the juice to darken his skin, so that he could smuggle himself in to see her Majesty.

As we stood there, Mary asked me to pick up a tiny cutting from the earth beneath the tree, and I managed to salvage a tiny two inch cutting with maybe one inch of root and on her Majesty's instructions I smuggled it out with me, and cared for it, as if our lives depended on it.

First I stored it in a open water bottle until I got it to our greenhouse a hundred miles to the south, where in some good potting compost and lots of water, it eventually took hold and started to sprout. I didn't know what is because no one could tell me. It is clearly a fruit bush similar to a gooseberry with long branches and dark green leaves, which are protected by sharp spines to prevent any unauthorised person enjoying the fruit.
It is not known in England and I can only guess that it is a fruit native to Scotland, maybe a Loganberry which Mary had sent down to her from Scotland.

"Nurture it well till I see you again" she commanded, " and bring it to me when you next visit me. And so I watered it every day, and it had pride of place on the window shelf of my office. It has flourished and there are three main tendrils which spread out from the centre.

I placed it very carefully on the floor of the passenger seat of the car and put the main tendril up towards the dashboard with the other two comfortable on the carpet. The main tendril kept tickling the place where the radio is and I had to adjust it so that it didn't move too much during the journey.

I caused some amusement in the hotel when I asked permission to bring in my plant, and Toni the receptionist seemed amazed but had no objections. So I carried Mary's plant to sit on the mantelpiece above the fireplace right next door to the main portrait of Mary. I carefully allowed the main tendril to sit upright and the other two to fall just over the edge of the mantelpiece. It looked settled and in place and I went to fetch a glass of water to refresh Mary's plant after its journey.

I loved the room, it was so friendly and had all the ambience of Mary and it was with some reluctance that I went out to explore the Town.
The buildings are stunning and seem to be taken for granted by the locals lucky enough to live there. I walked round and round, and was disappointed at first that all public buildings closed at 5pm, but I promised to revisit each one the next morning sharp at 10am when they were forecast to re-open.

I wanted to see the waters where Mary had taken them, but was amazed to find that the only remaining bath was a show bath in the middle of an arcade with a chair suspended over a tiny swimming pool maybe ten feet square. Here apparently old or crippled people could be placed in the chair and lowered into the warm water which is always at a very pleasant 27 degrees Whilst there is a sort of museum to the baths and this preserved example of one, their use was discontinued over thirty years ago much to my dismay.

I met a young man called Chris in the park and we chatted about Buxton. He told me with great pride of all the walks there were and said that I must go to Poole's Cavern because Mary Queen of Scots had visited. Again I knew I had to wait till the morning I gave Chris a copy of my book but having no pen I couldn't sign it until, quite half an hour later, he came rushing across shouting "Jock" having seen in the cover of the book the name of my publishers JocknDoris!

I was happy to sign and he asked me if I had seen The Crescent, and I set off round the other side up a steep hill to where the magnificent Town Hall is situated. There you can see a magnificent semi-circular building in the style of Regent Street in London and just as impressive and majestic.
The building is built in a beautiful gentle arc of a smooth, smooth crescent both back and front and looks at first sight in impeccable condition. I hurried down to see what this wonderful building was and as I got closer was amazed to realise that it was unoccupied. A notice said that £1.5m had been spent by the Heritage

Commission on restoring the outside but nobody could find a use for it.

What a tragedy! I immediately started plans to develop a beautiful hotel called the Mary Queen of Scots Hotel where people from all over the world would come to take the waters.
Underneath The Tourist Information Office is where all the baths and springs used to be and there I determined they will be again, when the hotel is opened.

I had a local beer at the pub just outside the Opera House, and chatted to the locals there in the sunshine. I then went to the little bistro type restaurant where I enjoyed a tasty starter and finisher both named after Mary Queen of Scots. I was in my element.

And so to bed. I had laid out on the bed all sorts of welcoming things for Mary. Pictures and books and some nice underwear I am certain she would have been proud to wear. I laid open the lovely sachet of herbs and the lavendar fragrance filled the room. I went to sleep looking at her portrait on the mantelpiece next to the plant I had brought for her.
During the night she came to me in the crook of my arm, just as my faithful cat Jock always does, and we roamed together through all the places we have met and she told me how pleased she was that I had grown the plant. She told me that the leaves are very helpful as a relief for her arthritis, and that she would gather a few of the leaves and put then inside her mittens or gloves, and the juices from the leaves would enter her skin and ease her pain.

"You must bring the plant with you when you come to Scotland", she told me, "and then it may be big enough for me to pick some leaves. I will see you when you have won your golf.", she said with confidence, "and then we must plan for Scotland's future."
"You will play one of my descendants, who is quite good, so you must be on your mettle to beat him" "Is he a Prince?" I asked. "Yes, I think so" she said.

We recalled happy memories of France and the chateaux with ornate walled gardens. Mary loves walled gardens possibly because those are the only ones she ever was allowed to wander freely in.

The only frightening experience was when we were under ground and under water in a horrible wet place where we couldn't find the way out. I was frightened not only because I couldn't find the way out, but because I was letting down my wonderful mistress, but we were whisked from there to Loch Leven and then back to Wingfield in a whistle stop tour of memories.

I woke up in the early light to look up with great affection at the portrait of Mary, when I noticed her left hand move to caress the tendril of the plant, which had by now grown across towards Mary's hand. I could not believe how there could be so much growth in such a short time, and Mary seemed to be coaxing and encouraging the plant to grow, such was the magnetism of this amazing woman.

When I got up in the morning and closely examined the plant, all the tendrils had grown two or three inches of new shoots. You could see the new growth as much lighter in colour than the rest of the plant. The main tendril was bent right over alongside Mary's left hand, which shows in the portrait the tell tale signs of arthritis - the slight swelling of the joints and the fingers slightly curled and apart. I showed the plant to Toni on reception and at least three of the ladies who came to Mary's Bower to get it ready for the next occupant They were all amazed at the growth and position of the main tendril.

It was then time for breakfast and as I waited for my traditional bacon and egg I walked to look at the rather impressive library on the walls. There stood a set of Sir Walter Scott's novels and my immediate thought was to look up the reference to Buxton in "The Abbot", but was very surprised to note that that one of the set was missing. I took this to mean I must look harder for the reference.

I then very carefully took Mary's plant back to the car for the return journey. As I placed it in exactly the same position as before, it was starkly clear that at least three inches had been added to the main tendril, as it now went well above the radio, and settled into a quite different position on the dashboard. On the way home I glanced at it from time to time to see if any new leaves appeared!
After breakfast I climbed the steep hill again to go to the Town Hall and there I asked to see whoever was responsible for The Crescent Building. "The Borough Treasurer can spare you five minutes" was the very friendly reply and I was ushered in to see Graham Sisson the Borough Treasurer.

"Unfortunately I have go to have something done to my knee in a few minutes but how can I help you?" he said. I told him I was here to see Mary Queen of Scots, but that I was amazed that such a wonderful building as The Crescent could be unoccupied. He then amazed me by saying they had discussed for five hours only the previous day (just before I arrived in Buxton) the whole future of the building, and that there was really no practical way they could do anything, much as they all wanted to.

I then suggested my idea of a hotel complex in Mary's honour opening up the baths again and drawing in tourists from all over the globe once our website was fully operational. He was excited and asked how can we fund it and I said that

Richard Branson was the man just taking over the lottery and this was perfect for lottery funding. We agreed that I would put a plan together, and I set off in exhilarated mood with ideas buzzing through my head. We exchanged cards and agreed to get in touch again once he had read my book.

I then set off for the Poole's Cavern only a mile away and as I had Mary's plant with me I planned to park the car in the shade and had to zigzag in the car park until I found the perfect spot facing the way I had come for a smooth takeoff.
I went into the reception area and at the desk I met a young man called Alan Walker and we got into conversation very easily. I explained I particularly wanted to see the spot where Mary Queen of Scots had visited. He said that the guided tour was already halfway round, but he would take me in a few minutes. He invited me into the little office where I met Suzanne and the rest of the staff.

"I can take you now" said Alan and we set off for the mouth of the cavern. It was hot out in the sunshine and as soon as we reached the double opening of the cavern it seemed to get much cooler.

We had to stoop under a four foot six ceiling, which Alan told me would have been much lower in Mary's day, almost making her have to crawl in under. I didn't enjoy the feeling at all as I am a little claustrophobic, and it was a shock when I saw the size and extent of the caves within. I had seen the exact view so many times before in my dreams with Mary! This was exactly the spot where Mary had asked me to help her get out, and I could not do so, and I had a terrible mixture of fear and exhilaration as I walked with Alan, terrified that I would lose touch with him.

I explained it to him and he was both sympathetic and understanding and I think a little excited too. We walked right up to the very far end of the cavern stopping only at the spot where Mary stood which is now known as Mary's pillar. It was incredibly cold and I could sense Mary's presence there.
I shouted up into the high high ceiling saying "Don't worry, Mary Queen of Scots, I now know the way out and Alan here will always show you if you ask him."
She replied in French saying she no longer had fear and a huge weight lifted off my shoulders and I too had no more fear. We came out into the sunshine after I had insisted on kneeling down to the old height to crawl out with no fear at all.

We told all to Suzanne and I promised to contact Alan if ever I wanted to explore any tunnels as he is an expert potholer.
I set off back to Mamble having had a exhilarating 24 hours with so much to look forward to, as I plan to see Mary again in Scotland in September at St Andrews.

St Andrews
Two Marys at the Jubilee Vase

I have tried to win the Jubilee Vase at St Andrews for thirty years, and have been very close twice before.
Maybe this year I can win for Mary Queen of Scots, who has told me she will appear after I have won, but surely she must be there to see if I do win.

The Jubilee Vase is the premier Handicap singles golf competition at St Andrews open only to full members of The Royal & Ancient Golf Club and as such has got to be one of the most coveted golf trophies in that illustrious trophy room at St Andrews. It sits proudly with the Open Claret jug and the Walker Cup when it is the UK's turn to hold it.

Alongside the Calcutta Cup, the twin of the England v Scotland rugby trophy, which are both made from melted down rupees, the Jubilee Vase is a majestic trophy in the shape of huge vase made of gold. It rarely comes out of the famous cabinet only to have the winner's name engraved upon it. No winner that I have known has held it aloft. It is far too heavy and too valuable, but we all fight tooth and nail to win it each year.

When I first entered I was a youngster of twenty five, and playing good golf off a handicap of 2. My home club was Royal Cape in Cape Town, South Africa and I travelled every year to play in the Jubilee Vase in September. In those days there was a simple draw on a knock out basis but with the very subtle rule that when matches were halved both players went forward! This meant that if you were all square with one to go that you did not try too hard to win the last hole because both players go forward if halved Also once you got to be dormie up, then you knew you must go forward, so the tendency to relax and let the match slip is understandable.

This was all great fun in the early rounds, but most annoying later if you have worked your socks off to beat one of your opponents, and two of your deadly rivals punched themselves to a standstill and halved their match so they both go through to the next round.
Of course there was no last sixteen or last eight as in most other knockout competitions, because if one couple halved there was bound to be an odd number and one lucky chap would go forward into the last seventeen!
Once I got to the last three players left in and the other two rascals halved their match so whereas yesterday I thought I was in the final, now I had to play one of the others for that right!

This sometimes meant that the competition went on too long and couldn't be finished in time so the committee reluctantly decided that all matches must finish under sudden death conditions i.e. the first person to lose a hole in extra play is eliminated. Sometimes these matches become very toothy in that you see your chance to win and then just can't take it, and you let your opponent off, hoping against hope that he will inadvertently return the favour at the next hole.

Now of course you know exactly when each round will be played including the semi-final and final so I just hope that Mary Queen of Scots can plan her trip accordingly.

I have seen many ghosts many times and have found that you must give them a welcoming signal, that they are both expected, and most definitely welcome.

I have found that Mary, who had four handmaidens all of whom were also called Mary, always feels welcome if one of her other Marys is there to greet her. So to encourage Mary Queen of Scots, I asked a friend of mine, called Sarah, to dress in the period costume of a long flowing dress and cap, to follow me round as a signal to Mary that she was expected and welcome.

I had a few splendid struggles in the early rounds, coming close to disaster at least twice, but I got through to the later stages and on the Thursday quarter final realised that if I won I might play Donald Galbraith in the semi-final if he, too, won his match. We had played once before some years ago and I know he wanted his revenge so it was an added incentive for me to win.
I was very tired, not the desperately tired I sometimes was when playing a second tense hard round of golf in a day, but we were locked at all square for the last few holes. I was dreading the nineteenth and sudden death, when at the seventeenth green I saw a tall elegant figure just behind the few spectators watching our match.
I was encouraged because this was my friend Sarah dressed as Mary and I knew she was on my side. I holed a long putt on the seventeenth to win the hole and put my second shot stone dead at the last to win two holes. It is easy if you have some encouragement.
When I got back to the hotel I went to see Sarah who surprised me by still being in bed poorly - "Sorry", she said, "I couldn't come out this afternoon - I got a tummy bug - how did it go?".
The hairs on the back of my neck went up, as I realised that the tall elegant figure watching me was not my friend Sarah. Who could it have been?

Sure enough it was Donald Galbraith in the semi-final and to add just that extra flavour in the other semi- final the pair included Prince Andrew destined to be the next royal Captain of the Club. He drove off first amid a lot of extra security and we followed a full quarter of an hour behind to give us all room to breathe.

I had asked Sarah to appear around the fourteenth hole near the end of the round, and so I was again puzzled to see, much earlier, the tall elegant figure always half a hole ahead of us waiting till she saw our shots, and then smoothly and swiftly moving on.

I began to tingle because my golf was the best it has been for years and I was receiving a few shots from Galbraith who is a much lower handicap than myself, presumably because he plays regularly through out the world. All I had I to do was concentrate and be calm, and I was in the final possibly against Prince Andrew who is of course a direct descendant of Mary Queen of Scots.

As we approached the fourteenth I was two up, (the dreaded two up with five to play) and had a stroke at the fourteenth. Just as I was about to drive I saw Sarah appear in her long flowing dress on the right hand side, and in the distance was my real Mary near the green.

When Galbraith very tactfully said "Did you know the Sky cameras are here today - it must be to catch Prince Andrew", that my concentration wavered a happenny, and although I hit it well my drive sailed straight into the dreaded Beardies, a set of small bunkers to be avoided at all costs.

Galbraith took his chance and hit a majestic drive down the right hand side and took the initiative.
Of course I had an appalling lie and had to hit backwards, and took four to reach Hell bunker with Galbraith sailing over up to the green. The hole was lost.

On the Fifteenth tee Galbraith announced "back to one" and I heard a voice say "One hole up is enough young Anthony" and I felt the prickles go up again, up the back of my neck. We had four holes to go and at each one Galbraith looked as if he would win. At the fifteenth I chipped from a long way out stone dead for a half. At the sixteenth Galbraith was three feet from the pin and, with two tall figures watching, I held my nerve and went for the long putt right into the back of the hole. Still one up and two to go.

The seventeenth is the dreaded Road Hole with a road right behind the green and it is disastrous to go over. It is equally dreadful to go left, because there is a very deep bunker only twelve feet from the hole.
Short and right is the place to be and that is where I was, ready to chip up for a four.

My faithful caddy Brian Martin has supported me throughout, and he was encouraging me to chip up close when a voice in my ear said "you must goforit, young Anthony" and I could already imagine Galbraith holing his putt for a three.

I got Brian to hold the flag and as I hit the chip I knew it was going straight in to the hole. Galbraith had now to hole his putt for a three to save the match, and as he lined up his putt there was a cheer from the eighteenth, as Prince Andrew clinched his match with a good putt. Galbraith did really well to compose himself, and hole the longish putt to force the game to the eighteenth.

We both hit good drives amongst all sorts of excitement, and I could see both Mary's within a few feet of one another as we walked up the fairway. Of course the small gallery watching Prince Andrew spread out to let us play through, but stayed to see my famous opponent play a glorious iron to the green rolling round to finish just six inches from the hole.

My stomach churned as I steadied myself with a couple of Klamath Lake Algae capsules, for some instant protein and a voice close to me said, "you can do it, young Anthony - because I want you to play one of my family tomorrow."

I said to Brian that to pitch it high would leave too much to chance, and so I took my favourite five iron down the shaft and ran it all the way along the ground through the 'valley of sin' up towards the hole. I couldn't see the ball finish, but the applause and then the cheer told me it was close.

I was inside Galbraith's ball, only three inches from the hole and he came over and gave me a bear-hug saying "you bugger - that was a great shot." I had won by one hole.

With that a number of people came up to congratulate me including Prince Andrew, and a tall elegant lady who said "you two will be playing tomorrow, I understand". I said, "Prince Andrew, you may not recognise your famous ancestor, Mary Queen of Scots, but she has been watching our matches closely today".
"I have been most impressed with the standard of play," she said "and the determination you have both shown. I was supporting (and helping did I hear) you both today, because I wanted you both to win so much. I cannot be with you tomorrow, because I would not know who to support," said her majesty.
"Have you met Donald Galbraith, your Majesty? I am sure you agree he was a worthy opponent".
"This is Mary Queen of Scots, Donald who I would like you to meet" as I

effected an introduction.

As he opened his mouth to speak, he caught my Sarah giving him a huge smile, so that he knew there were two Marys there.

"He was inspired today, your Majesty as anyone would be with you to support him. I accept defeat from a truly worthy opponent", said Donald.

"Please walk with me young Anthony", said she, and we strode off up the steps up past the R&A and up the Scores. "I will see you at Nether Kinnedar tomorrow at the feast" said she, "meanwhile your young Mary can look after me."

As I returned to the club to the beaming Brian, "you played well today young sir, but who was that wonderful lady?" "That Brian was none other than Mary Queen of Scots - watch her on Sky tonight and you will see two Marys! - one was Sarah who came with me as a friend, and the other was my wonderful Mary Queen of Scots.", I replied.

How could the final cap that - only time will tell!!

Sheffield Manor
A birching for a Queen

One day I recall returning with great joy to the Sheffield Tower having found a positive trove of dry logs and I was so pleased that I barged straight in to Queen Mary's room without announcing myself.

She was standing in the corner being dressed by the other Mary's and I stood riveted to the spot as I took in the most beautiful of sights. Her Majesty wore only a pair of exquisite French style knickers which were bright cerise and made of silk with white ruffles on the edges made of lace. She wore stockings beneath which came to her mid thighs and were loosely tied to those glorious pants. Rather incongruously she wore stout shoes. She had her back to me and I could see the exquisite lines of her back and shoulders so tall and elegant, sweeping down to those pants which I shall remember for the rest of this life, and many of the next.

I was rooted to the spot and simply could not move, and then realised that the Queen and both her Marys were so absolutely engrossed in robing her, that they had not heard me enter.

I had to force myself to reverse backwards towards the door which fortunately had stayed open and I withdrew and held my breath. Only light banter came from the Marys, and as luck would have it, Mary's Secretary arrived and said "Let me go first", as he knocked on the door I had so recently shut.

"One moment if you please" cried a voice, and we stood discussing the weather as we waited only a few seconds, before the cry of "Her Majesty will see you now".

As I looked at her Majesty, regal and majestic in her pristine dress of black with ruffles and gloves in place, I could see right through all the layers of material to those glorious knickers of red silk and white lace beneath. Far from demeaning her in any way, it only made me worship her more, as it was my secret and would remain so.

The Marys seemed to perform all manner of services for her Majesty, as I am sure she did for them and one day I heard one of them say to the other, " she will need another birching soon as she is very restless".

I didn't know what they meant, but I was sorry to hear that that she was restless, and so I interrupted rather stupidly and asked the Marys what they meant. "It is none of your business, young Anthony, but you had better behave otherwise our Queen will give you another hiding you deserve".

I said, " Nonsense - I have kept the fire going wonderfully well with fresh dry logs, and I have delivered all her letters on the right day to where they were supposed to go". "Can't you see that that is just what she doesn't want all the time - otherwise life is so dull - giving you a smacked bottom is a welcome distraction!!" said Mary Livingston.
Well I was amazed at this and pondered what Mary Livingston had said.
"Do you think I should be naughty on purpose just to please her majesty?" I asked. "Absolutely right - she is naughty sometimes and we have to smack her!!" said Mary
"I don't believe you Mary Livingston," I said almost trembling with excitement. Was it possible that my Queen liked being spanked just like me? - I suppose everything is possible.
"Why did you say that her Majesty needed to be birched?", I asked rather naively, and Mary Seton said "it is for her circulation - it brings the blood to the surface and improves the circulation. Lord Bothwell taught her to do it as he had learnt it in the Scandinavian countries".
"Is it not sore?" I asked. "Not if you do it gently to start with, and then build up harder, which is what Her Majesty loves - but if you tell anyone ever, I will tell her Majesty all the dreadful things you have done - ever!" said Mary Livingstone.

I went away with my mind boiling with thoughts of my wonderful Queen being birched and loving it.
The next time I saw her Majesty on her own was two days following, and she had been a little ill tempered of late, and said to me "Young Anthony - what mischief have you been up to, and have not told your Queen about?".   This I recognised as an invitation to own up to something which could lead to a spanking that I enjoyed so much.

Without giving it any further thought, I blurted out, "Your Majesty I came in here three days ago, and forgot to knock and I saw you being dressed by the Marys - You looked beautiful, and I can remember perfectly how you looked even now. I am ever so sorry because I didn't mean to, but what I saw was the most beautiful thing I will ever see!"

"And what did you see young Anthony - be very careful because if you are fibbing just to get a spanking I will know. What did you see?", said Mary Queen of Scots, hoping against hope that he had not seen anything he shouldn't have seen.

"Your Majesty I saw your wonderful red knickers with white frills, and they were so beautiful and your stockings too, which I have never seen before", said I, walking straight into the biggest thrashing of my life.

"Young Anthony it is I, your Queen, who should be ashamed wearing such extravagant and frivolous clothes that I deserve to be punished not you - will you help me expunge that by birching me severely?", said her Majesty.

I could not believe my ears.

"And I will bear it with fortitude because I have sinned terribly, and you have been good not to tell anyone, as the Marys would have told me, had that been so" she said.

"What would you have me do?" I asked in trepidation.

With that Mary Queen of Scots walked across the room to a cupboard, and withdrew a bundle of birch twigs, very thin and whippy - all bound at one end into a handle made of leather, and handed them to young Anthony.

"What you saw a few days ago young Anthony, was the Marys checking my back to make sure no marks remained from my last birching, and whether I was allowed to have my next one, which is of course for medicinal purposes you know" said her Majesty.

"I shall lie over this stool, and you must forget I am your Queen, and you must lift up all my skirts and unbutton all my blouses, till you can see my bare back! Then, young Anthony, you must birch me as hard as you can, forgetting that I am your Queen " she commanded.

Before I could stop her, even if I had wanted to, she flung herself over her embroidery stool placing her tummy on its embroidered seat, and said " I am waiting young Anthony - do as you must - I command you".

I moved forward in a haze of euphoria and excitement, yet fearing that the end of the world was at hand. Her Majesty had buttons all down the back, and as I fumbled with the top ones, she settled more into the stool until I had exposed all her back. Her head was so far forward that her cap was touching the floor to reveal the back of her lovely neck. I could see underneath her own hair was very dark and very short. "You must start now young Anthony " she cried. I caught just a glimpse of those unbelievable red pants and that was enough to bolster my courage to the limit.

"You are not yet fully prepared, Your Majesty," said I, as I continued with the buttons further and further down until her skirts fell apart to reveal all of her wonderful body. I was now within inches of my wonderful Queen and wanted to kiss her and worship her all over but this was not my instruction.

"Your Majesty I am commanded by yourself to birch you, and that I will commence any second but because you have brazenly worn the most provocative of French underwear, I propose to birch you over these panties as well". I said, with as much authority as I could.

"Are you ready Your Majesty?", I asked.

"Mary Queen of Scots is always ready - do you hardest, young Anthony, in service to your Queen", was her royal instruction.

I started first by laying the birch down across her shoulders, very gently to show her the spot, and I brought the birch down with medium force, which hardly caused a movement from the Queen.

I did four or five of similar strength, and already could see the redness appear across her shoulders and down her back. I increased the intensity slowly, until I was breathing heavily with the exertion and I noticed her Majesty driving her tummy into the stool, whilst her legs were pushing slightly apart.

I stepped up the tempo and she started to stand on tiptoe, and this caused me to whack her for the first time across those royal knickers.

She exclaimed, not out of pain or surprise, but sheer pleasure, shouting "how dare you hit me there" with which I hit her there again, and she brought her knees forward and apart raising her bottom as an irresistible target.

I brought the twigs down time and again across each buttock, and across the top on each hip and each time she grunted and gasped in pleasure. I had not noticed where she had put her hands before, but something stirred underneath her pants as he she moaned and moaned.

"Do you not think that the rest of the punishment should be centred on these red knickers which seem to have caused all the trouble", her Majesty asked, although I sensed her concentration was wavering and her thoughts fixed elsewhere.

"I must finish the punishment off correctly, Your Majesty", I announced. "You will have a further twelve strokes with the birch, six on each side of those red knickers. I wish you count out the strokes with the number and thank you young Anthony" and that she did in absolute raptures.

We never reached twelve, let alone six, as on number four she came in a shattering climax which befitted my most wonderful Queen.

I stopped and drew breath as she did. I soaked in the most beautiful sight of her majestic back, red and glowing and her bottom glued to those glorious pants of red silk and white lace, all of which was now a deeper shade of red caused by truly royal wetness.

I stood up and stood aside.

"You must button me up, Young Anthony   - anyone might see", and I started with fumbling fingers to button up her royal costume.

As I did up the last button, she stood up and turned in her regal way - still fully eight inches taller than I, and said "Thank you, young Anthony, you have today done your Queen a real service - for which I am truly grateful".

With that there was a knock on the door, and her Majesty said in a loud voice, "Make sure you keep that fire properly fed with logs, young Anthony Babington, otherwise I will have to deal with you again".   As the others came in they took the flush on my cheeks as that of embarrassment at having just been dealt with by Her Majesty, and her flush as that of exertion in so doing.

But both Mary Queen of Scots and I know better.

Wingfield Manor
Show me the way to go home

As the new Treasurer of the Marie Stuart Society I set off early to Ashby de la Zouche for our meeting to see the Castle there. Due at 10.30am I tried to set off early, but had to meet Jan at Stourport to arrange the finishing touches to the cap and veil that I had ordered for Mary Queen of Scots.

I set off for Ashby and found it very easily in an incident free journey, but when I got there I found only one car park and the only space was a disabled driver's one. I used it as there did not appear to be any disabled people looking for a space. As I walked up the drive to the Ashby de la Zouche Castle, I discovered there was a small car park there and moved the car to a relaxed spot just beside the gate.

A miserable day with fairly consistent drizzle but Keith Cheetham was there ready to cheer us up.

We went inside the cabin where two girls in identical outfits of grey trousers and tops with the English Heritage logo of a square castle motif. I couldn't help wondering if they had matching bra and panties which would have looked sensational with the castle motif all over them - one girl Georgi was very pretty indeed with a charming smile of white teeth.

The visit was dull to say the least because the Walkmans were very poor and didn't hold your attention and most of us went our own ways.

I asked the girls in the cabin how to get to Wingfield Manor as I wished to visit Mary there - exit 29 they said on the M1 and they were close, as exit 28 was the right answer!

I set off having to get petrol just after exit 28 and as I came off at exit 29, I spotted a sign which tempted me to go to Hardwick Hall - the magnificent home of the Earl of Shrewsbury and Bess of Hardwick who were Mary's jailers for fourteen years. I had to stop at a car park gateway and was robbed of £2 for a ticket by a man who did not know if Mary Queen of Scots had ever been there.

I drove what seemed two miles up a long meandering single track drive and was parked by two attendants in yellow jackets who also did not know if Mary had ever been there.

I was getting grumpy as I walked to the front gate where some over-cheerful foreigners were parting with £10 each for the privilege of seeing the Hall, which in all fairness is magnificent, but clearly not the one in which Mary was imprisoned as it was only started in 1657.

I was not duped into paying any more fees as I about-turned and drove the car another two miles on the one way system to eventually get out.   I had the feeling of having escaped the clutches of an octopus.

I retraced my steps and went where I should have gone the first time, and went through North Wingfield and then Crich pronounced Kr (eye) Ch ,where a marvellous character in the service station who had a cheeky grin just like Ernest Borgnine's, directed me past the Greyhound pub and keep right on down the hill and up again, and would have given me many more directions when I stopped him telling him I couldn't remember any more all at once.

"Turn right and you can't miss it", said the man in the next pub and sure enough there was Wingfield Manor high up on the hilltop.   It took another two miles to circum-surround it, and at the bottom of the hill were signs clearly saying 'No unauthorised vehicle allowed'.   I didn't let this deter me, and got right up to the top of the quite steep hill, and parked immediately outside the cabin.

I went in to meet the charming lady called Gill who told me very politely that I couldn't park there.   I told her equally politely that I couldn't possibly walk up the hill again, and asked for a ticket!

This time the Walkman was magnificent - being about two foot six long and easy to hold with the earpiece at the end. I followed the whole tour round and began to become engrossed in the remarkable building - all really driven by a huge kitchen with two enormous open fires with massive chimneys, and certainly from the walkman, the whole Manor seemed to have been a wonderful eating house.

Mary had of course been imprisoned here for three months and it was from there that Anthony Babington had planned to rescue her by way of an underground tunnel leading back to his Manor Farm which Isabel Uttley called Thackers Farm in her wonderful best seller 'A Traveller in Time'.

I was irritated by some young boys from a big group there swordfighting, and so I went outside and saw a small doorway into a huge underground chamber which I later found out was called the Undercroft. It was immediately eerie, not only because it was dark but also because it had pillars with archways between them, which all met at the top making sixteen or so individual underground chambers.

The floor was dry gravel so you could hear yourself walk and I was immediately on alert. At the far end was a tiny archway set in the floor coming only to about knee height. There was an square opening maybe eighteen inches deep, obviously intended for someone to descend but of course it went nowhere, and as I peered into it and was clearing some logs and sticks there, I heard a familiar voice say "that is where Anthony was going to rescue me, but they got to him before he could do so".

Mary Queen of Scots then came and sat beside me, with her feet in the opening and we talked for what seemed ten minutes or so in total seclusion, and she told me of her disappointment at not being rescued, and how our efforts must be re-doubled, as all the tunnels were now finished and all they had to do was breakthrough here.

"I will tell them", I told her Majesty, and she said, "go to the farm this very afternoon, and you will find they are still labouring on the tunnels.   I will be brave, and can fit though any hole that his men can create."

At that point children and others burst in though the door I had used, and Mary was gone without really finishing what she had told me.

I was frustrated but felt elated too as I had been in the presence of Mary for the longest period yet.

What a wonderful person she is - so graceful and glamorous at the same time - able to stun me with her beauty even in the darkness of an underground chamber.

Later as I stood by the huge old walnut tree in the courtyard, Mary asked me to pick up a sapling and to nurture it well till I saw her next.

When I got back to the cabin I told Gill how wonderful the trip had been and how elated I was and how I had seen Mary and she was amazed saying, "Did you know that we are starting a ghost tour here today?"   Richard has just taken out the first group.

Well I was amazed as well and left her my number and a book to call me if anything happened.

Babington Farm
Uncle Barnabas

I left in great spirits to try and find the Babington Manor Farm and at the bottom of the hill asked a very nice lady called Audrey Buxton from Oundle if she knew the way.

"Take the road to Crich", she said and I turned left and set off.

I found Crich and then Holloway and as I approached Lea I stopped at a Butcher's to ask a young man called John Maycock, with a full pair of ears, for directions to Thackers Farm.

He asked his father and it was only when I mentioned the Babington's that he said "you need to find Dethick, which is a hamlet with three farms and a Church". He gave me clear directions including zigzagging across a junction across the main road as I climbed the hill to Dethick.

Again 'no parking' signs everywhere which puzzled me, but there was a wedding on at the church and so I joined in and parked in the wedding party's car park.

Outside the top of the path to the church was a Rolls Royce with the mandatory ribbons and smartly dressed driver. I told him I was nothing to do with the wedding but had just met Mary Queen of Scots who told me to come and seek out Thackers Farm.

There it was as large as life with Babington Farm and Manor Farm clearly shown, and I explored the outbuildings, quietly nodding to the occasional wedding guest, as the service seemed just to have finished.

I walked down the little path carefully closing the gate behind me, and watched the wedding photographs being taken and the guests shivering in their mandatory too thin dresses which I always find very fetching.

Eventually all the wedding party left, and I walked gently into the church where the vicar and a lady stood. The vicar was just like the one in 'keeping up appearances', young and good-looking, very fresh and wholesome. I explained that I was nothing to do with the wedding party and just happened to be there by chance and as they seemed interested, I told them of seeing Mary.

I prefaced everything by saying that I didn't wish to offend anyone and they could throw me out anytime.

Both he and Nancye, who turned out to be the organist, seemed very interested with Nancye first suggesting that the Mary I saw was the one they had dressed up for a pageant in Derby, but I said I knew the girl called Julie and it wasn't her, but the real Mary Queen of Scots.

When I asked the vicar, whose name I never discovered, whether he believed in ghosts, he started talking but what came out was wishy-washy nonsense as if he was very flustered.

I said that I would like to know the middle initial of Anthony Babington and Nancye said that I must go with her as she could tell me. Later the vicar's wife arrived at the church.

Eventually we tidied up ready to go, and I said I had one book left in the car which I would like him to have, and I would go and fetch it from the car seeing them both at the top of the lane.

As I rushed to the car, I passed the Manor Farm house, where a splendid man, probably in his eighties, had just appeared with an arm crutch to help him walk. I waved to him and asked him if this was the famous farmhouse in Alison Uttley's book and he beamed with pride and said "would you like to see it?"

I whooped with joy and we set off down a little corridor and there I saw the most amazing room with three enormous arches on one side, the middle one had a modern fireplace with a canopy over it. It had clearly been an enormous open fireplace in the old days, as described in great detail by Alison Uttley with the serving boys turning a huge roast on a spit basting it with oils from a bowl at the side.

The other arches on either side had been converted for tables but their original use was clear.
We turned to the long table with dominated the middle of the room and you could almost see the people sitting there ready to eat a wonderful meal.

I thanked him warmly and asked his name which he gave me, but when I signed the last book to give to him, I couldn't recall it even from two minutes ago and had to ask again.

I said, "you are not Uncle Barnabas are you?" and he stuttered and said "My name is Harold Groom" but he was a little shaken and before I could ask him more, both the vicar and Nancye came into the room.

"Our cars are causing an obstruction", the vicar declared, "we must move them before there is trouble", and although there were 'no parking' signs everywhere, there was equally no sign of anyone else and certainly no sign of any trouble. I told Mr Groom that he must ring me if anything happened and I was outside the house walking towards the cars.

The vicar was really flustered now, whether egged on by his timid wife I do not know, but was concerned and said, "please do not bother Nancye any further", and got into the car and drove off.

I was in a quandary. I wanted to go and see Nancye and Mr Groom again, mainly to say goodbye but I didn't want to overstay my welcome, or distress anyone so I backed the car up to outside the farm house and waited a few minutes hoping Nancye would come out.

But she didn't although she must have seen me.

Who was she do you think? and was Mr Groom really Uncle Barnabas?

Only time will allow me to discover.

I will write to her and see.

I left and had a lovely journey back.

What an extraordinary plant
A cure for Mary's arthritis

I was keen to find out more about the plant that I had nurtured for Mary Queen of Scots.

So I took it one day to Countryside Nurseries near Stourport where I knew they would know what it was. There were now five strong tendrils each having sharp spikes protecting the rich green leaves. It looked like a fruit bush of some kind but what variety and why had Mary asked me to nurture it for her? When I showed it to Graham he had a puzzled look on his face as if to say, "I have never seen that before but Bill is bound to know! Leave me a piece and I will ask him when he is in tomorrow. We will try and get the stem to root for you in the meantime."

A couple of days later I got a call from Nicky, the owner of the Nursery, to say that her father Bill was sure he had never seen the plant before. "Not found in England I would say, but if you want to be sure - contact the Natural History Museum. They are the established authority on it."

So I phoned Directory Inquiries to get the number and the girl unfortunately looked up National History and of course could find nothing. Eventually she got me the number and I phoned with a little trepidation, because it was only a small fruit bush and they probably wouldn't be remotely interested.
I spoke to chap who said, "There is only one man who could answer your questions with any authority- and that is Reg Vicary the curator, but he is far too busy to be bothered with the likes of you!"
That put me firmly in my place, but I persevered and said, "How much of the plant do you need?"
"About six inches" was the reply.
"I've only got about that amount left" I said and so he said "send as much as you can".
"Where to?" I asked
"The Natural History Museum, London" was the reply.
"What street" I asked and with absolute confidence he said, "No street address is required just the Natural History Museum, London will do!"
"The Post Code?", I thought surely.
"Can't be bothered with those things," he said "complete waste of time!"

Well I cut as long a piece as I dared, and put it in a plastic folder and padded envelope, addressed to the Natural History Museum and held my breath.

Nothing happened for ten days or so and then the phone went and a voice said "Reg Vicary here can I please speak to Neil Burns? We are very interested in your plant", he said, "but we don't believe a word of your story. That plant is never found in England at all and you couldn't have found it at Wingfield Manor, as it is only found on the West Coast of Scotland."

"It is a wild gooseberry. It very rarely propagates itself, because in nature it has to smother all other plants around it to survive, just as a bramble does, and so it also smothers its own young, so your story of picking up a sapling or cutting is not on!", said Reg Vicary.

Well this made me very excited, and as I explained the story in more detail to him, it became obvious that the plant must have been sent down from the West of Scotland to Mary when she was at Wingfield Manor. The leaves of course would have helped soothe her arthritis.

And we both agreed that, if this was all there was left, then this must be the only remaining part of the plant which had to be over four hundred years old!

"We want to see the berries when they appear next year", said he, "as they will confirm exactly what is it is. Keep it carefully but don't molly coddle it, as it will be used to frost and snow and will, so to speak, hibernate over the winter."

I went up to St Andrews in September to play in the Jubilee Vase, and took the plant with me and kept it in my room much to the amazement and amusement of my landlady who said, "Why don't you take it to the Botanical Gardens? - They will know what it is". So I did and one of the curators there got very excited because he said that they very rarely see such a plant.

"Leave it with us for a while"

When I came back to collect it two days later one of the tendrils had disappeared and when challenged the man said "Oh we sent that to the man in Dundee - at the University - he wants to see if it has any medical qualities."

A fortnight later I got a phone call from a Dr Morely who was excited to say the least, saying "Those leaves you sent us contain a remedy used by homoeopaths for years for the relief of arthritis and rheumatism - I ought to know because I am the Professor here at Dundee - please may I have some of the berries when they appear next year - they will make a wonderful gel as a soothing balm."

Mary had told me that she had put the leaves under the fingers of her mittens and this was wonderful confirmation that what she had told me was true.

I can't wait for Spring and Summer because I must try to propagate from our bush and also see what medical benefits can be found from these berries when they appear.

This is the most concrete proof so far that my meetings with Mary are real and it may be that this is what she has been asking me to do.

* * * * *

Recently I had the privilege of going to see the Duke and Duchess of Devonshire at their stately home at Chatsworth. They were interested in my plan to re-open the spa at Buxton which was built by the fifth Duke. They were also very interested in the plant and I have suggested to them that it should have a special place in Mary's Bower which is an extraordinary tower garden that was built for her in 1570 with a moat round it supposedly to keep her in captivity. I have offered to re-design the garden in the shape of Mary's face and put the wild gooseberry right in the centre at the top as the jewel in her crown - maybe this will encourage Mary to return there, as she will know that the aid to her arthritis will be to hand.

Rescuing a Snow Queen
Back to Nether Kinnedar

I lived during the seventies in a wonderful little village called Saline in Scotland, where you will recall I met Sir Walter Scott, and that in turn was close to Stirling, which used to be the main castle fortress of Scotland and some say the real Capital.

Those of you who have read "A few special GHOSTS I have met" will remember that I have a Visitors Book in my car and all people to whom I give a lift are invited to sign. One man who I saved from the snow however, could neither read nor write and I had to sign his name for him. He was delighted because he had never seen his name in writing before.

I now have five further entries in my visitors' book, which are intriguing!

When I was on one of my regular visits to Scotland it turned very very cold, with heavy snow falls in the central region. I was on my way to visit friends near Stirling along the country roads which are narrow, twisty and in places very steep - not the place to be driving when it starts to snow.

I drove as carefully as I could until I was approaching my home town of Saline up the infamous Comrie road, when it became too slippy to get enough grip and I realised that I could go no further. I looked for a suitable place to park the car, remembering that some years ago my friend Jack Romanes had parked his car up at Phil Inch's farm ready to play a game of Bridge, and hadn't seen it for another three weeks as it, and everything else, was buried in snow.

This was the first snow of the season and it was unexpected and seemed to have caught many people out including me. I don't listen to the radio so had no warning of it. I knew I was just half a mile from Saline and another half mile to get home so I saw the little lay-by beside the cottages at Comrie and parked there.

As always I was wearing my famous green coat which is in the style that Sherlock Holmes (and Douglas Herd) used to wear. It has a wonderful fleecy lining, so I knew I would be warm and it was going to be quite exciting to walk the mile to Preston Place. It was going to be slippy though, so I got out of the car and opened the boot to find my golfing shoes which would ensure I had a nice grip as the road got steeper.

As I was putting them on I heard some excited voices, "Maybe that fine gentleman can help us?" "What is he doing do you think?" and I turned round to see four figures all wrapped up against the cold but shivering nevertheless and I exclaimed "whatever are you doing out in this dreadful snow?"

"We were running an errand for our mistress but we got lost and cannot find the way back to the house", said one of them. "First we must get you warm", I said - and opened the doors of the car. "It will be warmer inside".
At first they were very hesitant, looking as if they were actually afraid of the car - the very thing that could offer them warmth and safety.   They were shivering and looking very pale indeed and I inquired "what in the world of goodness are you doing out on a dreadful day such as this?"
"We have got lost and we cannot find our Queen - she is left behind" said one of the girls all of whom were wearing long dresses to the ground with heavy woollen capes and old fashioned caps, which covered their ears.

"The car is warm and I think you should climb aboard and we can talk in the car" I suggested. "We are very cold, kind sir, but we are also very afraid because we have never seen such a contraption as yours before", said one.

The Audi purred gently by the roadside and I opened the various doors and invited them to get in with a gentlemanly sweep of my arm. "We are frightened that you will drive off in the carriage and we do not know where you will take us!" one cried.

I suggested that if I stood outside then that could not happen and that did the trick! One by one they squeezed in to the car with two of them in the back and the tallest one in the front, and then another in the drivers seat.   I then stood shivering outside as the heater began its work in earnest. It is a great feeling when you have been chilled to the bone and then at last there is some heat to take the chill away and to take the pain out of your fingers and toes.

I stood by the driver's door and wound down the window so that I could talk to my new friends and asked them for their names. One by one they answered "Mary" and then the next said "Mary" and the third said "Mary" and the hairs on the back of my neck began to tingle.   Because around 1567 there were four girls all called Mary who attended the most famous Mary of all, Mary Queen of Scots.

Before the fourth could answer "Mary" I asked "but where is your mistress, where is your Queen?" and they burst into speech all together giving garbled explanations of where she might be.
Slowly I said, "where did you last see her?" and they said "We left her at Comrie with Lord Kincaird because she told us to!" And so I said, "we must find her

because she must be cold too!"

"She will be safe with Lord Kincaird", said a Mary.
"We shall see", said I, "because you have commandeered my vehicle we must go and find her."

The Mary who was in the driving seat had to be persuaded to come out of the warmth and squeeze into the back seat with the two others and I was beginning to wonder wherever we could fit anyone else into the already crowded car.

I climbed in and very gently eased the car forward to squeals of delight from the Marys. It seemed that nothing phased them so long as they were together and were doing their mistress's wishes.
Back towards Comrie was mainly downhill and wc slid and slippcd with mc trying to maintain control of the car as we descended through the very thick snow.

Windscreen wipers going flat out to try and keep a clear view. As we turned the corner into Comrie we saw Mary - Queen Mary walking slowly towards us along the roadside with a slight limp as if she had twisted her ankle.

We drew alongside with my heart pounding because here surely was my beloved Mary Queen of Scots who I had waited so long to meet, and I could surely be of service to her this time. I wound down the electric window for the Mary in the front to exclaim to her mistress " We are here, we are saved. Your Majesty, and we will make room for you!"

Mary in the front got out, as I did, and made way for Mary Queen of Scots who even in this most difficult of circumstances was regal and elegant and poised.

"Your Majesty I am proud to be able to be of service to you and your party," said I, hardly able to believe it was true. As she slid elegantly into the passenger seat, her tall cap touched the ceiling and her dark hair was slightly squashed but she looked most beautiful although very pale.

As we sat in the car the heater was going full blast, and I could see that Mary Queen of Scots had been very close to being frozen alive, as her eyebrows were frosted and all her cap and ruffles were covered in snow. As I watched her out of the corner of my eye I saw her visibly warming, with colour returning to her cheeks and saw her flexing her fingers to get the circulation back.

I told her of the Visitors book and asked if she would like to sign it and she said, "yes indeed I am happy to sign for any of my subjects, particularly if they save me from the snow and cold" and she signed there and then. She then insisted the four Marys sign as well which was difficult as all four were curled up in the back, but amidst giggles they quickly signed on the page below Mary's signature.

"We will stay here Your Majesty until you are warm, and then you must give me your instructions as to where we must go." I said.
"I would be safe in Stirling I know", she said, "so we ought to go there - or at Linlithgow Palace they are expecting me also, but where oh where will Bothwell be as this snow will hold him up also".

The Marys at the back were curled up one on each others laps and I could almost hear them purring they were so content and so happy that their Queen was safe.

Then I had a brainwave as I remembered that Nether Kineddar was very close at hand and I knew the owners very well. It was still only lunchtime, so we could probably join them for a bite to eat -the only problem was that it was steeply uphill and far too slippy to get the car up there.

"Your Majesty it is too dangerous, in my view, to drive in these conditions, and so with your safety uppermost in my mind, I suggest we walk a short distance where I will guide you to the home of a great friend of mine who will give us a warm welcome", I suggested.

"Who is this friend? Do I know him?", Her Majesty enquired and I said "The house used to owned by Lord Kineddar and is called Nether Kineddar in his honour. It will be most comfortable".

My guests were getting too comfortable in the warmth of the car which I could only sustain for a hour at most, so without further ado I switched the engine off and said, "Please follow me - if we hold hands we will stay together and not fall over."

With that, all climbed out of the car with a few begrumbles from the Marys and assembled in a line as I locked the car. "I shall lead, as I know the way and you Mary Seton will bring up the rear and will call to me that you are still there so that we are all accounted for", I instructed.

And so we set off for a walk that I had hoped would only take five minutes but we slipped and fell over slowing progress. But it was fun because it was fresh snow and all the party were young and enjoying themselves. I was surprised at the strength in my legs as I tugged them up the hill getting a good grip with my golf shoes.

Eventually we reached the road end for Nether Kineddar and saw a few cars there - they must have guests for lunch, which augured well. As the bedraggled snow-covered six reached the main driveway we could hear the sounds of revelry - Sue and Roddy must have be having a wonderful party or knew we were coming!

The front door has a majestic staircase that sweeps up to it and I suggested that the party wait at the foot as I went and announced ourselves. The door of course was open demonstrating the wonderful natural hospitality of Scottish people and I went in and called across to Roddy who was crossing the hall into the big lounge.

"Roddy I have some totally uninvited, but very exciting guests for you to meet - as I promised I would one day!" I said. "Oh yes" he said "is it Sir Walter Scott again?" - and I said "No - even more exciting - because Mary Queen of Scots and her party are outside - very cold but in good spirits and would enjoy the warmth of your fire."

"Bring them in - we are having an early Xmas party and Colin and Kitty are here!" said Roddy. "How wonderful" I replied and rushed out to escort Mary Queen of Scots up the staircase. Even covered in snow she looked elegant and regal, stunning in fact and I realised how tall she was, accentuated by her gathered hairstyle and regal head-dress.

She took my arm as I escorted her up the stairs and I let her go first through the doorway. There was a hush as the assembled Xmas party group were stunned by her appearance. I introduced "Your Majesty, this is Master Roddy Jones, our host and a good Scotsman", and Roddy for once was lost for words as I continued, "Roddy, this is Her Majesty, Mary Queen of Scots!"

Roddy recovered well by saying " We are honoured by your presence Your Majesty. Do please come in and bring your party with you". Roddy led Queen Mary towards the fireplace introducing her as he went to his wife Sue, to Colin McCrone and to Kitty McCrone and then their daughters Morag and Heather and their husbands.

I was surrounded by the four Marys and made it easy for everyone by saying, "These four lovely girls are all called Mary, as they are the royal attendants and companions of Her Majesty, Mary Queen of Scots!"
With that someone came from the kitchen with a tray of drinks which looked like hot mulled wine and all the Marys eagerly reached for a glass - the first one sipping and then passing it to her mistress.

Within seconds Mary Queen of Scots had taken centre stage and was in control and everyone was happy and getting warmer by the second. Quite what Roddy thought I didn't know - knowing as I did that Mary had ruled Scotland in 1567 but he was bowled over by the Queen as he stood by her side near the fireplace in his lounge beaming with pride.

The front room was warmed by an enormous fire and to stand too close to it one was in danger of catching fire oneself. There was a beautiful bay window with a curved window seat and I took the Queen's arm again and led her to sit in the centre of the bay window. The Queen was immediately joined by two of the Marys whilst the other two went straight to the kitchen in search of food for Her Majesty.

"What a wonderful spread you have laid on for us!" I said to Roddy, "We couldn't have asked for anything more. The wine is wonderful. What it is exactly?" "Red wine with a little rum and lots of cloves and good Scots water", was his reply - a Roddy Jones special!

At that moment Mary Livingstone arrived with two plates one for Mary Queen of Scots and one for me! I was truly honoured. Roddy brought a round table on which I had played many games of Bridge, and set it before us so that we could eat in comfort.

As Mary began to eat she warmly thanked Roddy and Sue for their hospitality and said how fortunate it had been that Master Burns should arrive to first rescue them and then escort them to his fine home.

"Neil has told us before of his admiration and devotion to you and has said many times if the opportunity arose he would bring you to meet us - how happy we are today that he has done so!" Roddy replied.

"Your majesty we are very lucky today to have two physicians in the party with us, and I think I saw you limping a little as we came up the road." I commented. "Yes. You are right. - I turned my ankle a little as I slipped - it would be most kind if your physicians could attend to me" said the Queen.

With that both Colin and Kitty came forward and Colin was charm personified as he asked to look at Mary's ankle. Her Majesty asked Mary Seton to lift her dress a fraction so Colin could find her ankle and I could see Kitty noting, with amazement, the old fashioned material used as leggings and hand knitted socks which tried to keep out the cold.

Colin reassured her that it was only a very slight strain and she must rest for a couple of days. But then asked to examine her hands and as he gently massaged her palms and fingers he noticed Mary Queen of Scots grimace just a happenny. "You are very astute young man", she said, "what do you think it is that causes my long fingers to ache and the joints to swell?"

"Your Majesty, I fear you have the beginnings of arthritis but if you take Rushhout sometimes called Poison Ivy then it will ease the pain and save you much trouble later in life." said her Doctor. Mary Livingstone made a note and was instructed to let Her Majesty have regular small doses of rushhook from then on.

The party continued as friends of Roddy's came to pay their respects and I knew that I must have a few minutes alone with the Queen.

I sought leave to sit on a small chair close to her and when my chance came, I said "Your Majesty I have long looked forward to meeting you and I am delighted to have done so today. I have however other services to provide for you. I cannot tell the future but I know many things and I must alert you to the dangers ahead. You know, I think, that your husband Lord Darnley has been seen many times in the inns of Edinburgh and he enjoys drinking and when his inhibitions are loosened he frequents various houses of ill repute!"

"Well your husband is not well and it seems clear that he will die of his illness in but a few months. Do not despair because this will be best for you. But be aware that he tries to incriminate you in a plot to murder him. He will try to lure you to Kirk o' Fields which has been specially chosen. There Lord Darnley plans to kill both himself and Your Majesty by blowing up the house with gunpowder. You would be best advised to send troops there first to discover the plot".

"Be most careful too about writing letters to Lord Bothwell that could be misunderstood as they will later come back to haunt you if they are in the wrong hands. If you are patient you will be free to marry again, once your beloved Bothwell is also free to marry. And you can rule here in Scotland until you deem it is time for your son James to become King of both Scotland and England. You must stay in Scotland and let the English come to you, not exhaust yourself and your troops by marching south of the border. How I wish I could be here at your side but I fear that is not possible!" I finished.

"Thank you, kind sir for those words of advice but I am at a loss to know how you can be so sure of events yet to come!" she exclaimed.

"All I ask is that you heed my words nearer the time, as they are the truth", I said.

Eventually it came time to leave as the dusk began to fall, and Roddy and I went out to see what the weather held to see a beautifully clear sky with white white snow on the ground as far as the eye could see but no biting wind - it was as fresh as fresh could be.

Roddy said "I have long wheel base Range Rover which holds the ground well and I am happy to put it at your disposal - it will seat six comfortably!" And with that he strode off to get it ready for us.

As the party began to leave each member bade farewell to Mary Queen of Scots and the four Marys who had also signed Sue and Roddy's visitors book, promised to come back again if at all possible.

As we set off I said, "Your Majesty, may I suggest Falkland Palace is closest - I know the way well - we can be there in an hour."
"Very well, young sir, let us drive your carriage to Falkland and maybe Lord Bothwell will be there to greet us" said Mary Queen of Scots.

I drove very carefully round the country roads knowing that I had a very valuable cargo indeed. We saw Falkland from a great distance and I glanced once at the petrol gauge as it flashed its warning that we were short of fuel, but it held and we took the gradual climb up the hill to the gates of the Palace.
There I announced to the guard that it was Her Majesty and he came forward with all due deference and as soon as he recognised her he swept open the gates to let us in.

The palace looked majestic as it should, with snow covering all the beautiful roofs and turrets, and we could see the lights from the fires shining though the stain glass windows which shone as it now was nearing dark.

The telltale signs of a fire flickering in the main hall reassured us all that a warm welcome awaited, and I suggested that everyone wait, until I go inside with the guard and announce our arrival.
He and I trod straight to the main gate and announced ourselves and the keeper of the Palace was summonsed.

When I returned with the same guard to the car we retraced our footsteps but found the car empty - totally empty - and as I looked back at the Palace there was Mary Queen of Scots and her four Marys inside waving to us to say thank you but there were no telltale footsteps in the snow!

"You must go now", said the guard rather unkindly, "you are no longer needed here" and I turned the car with a final wave and left down the drive.

The car got only as far as the bottom of the lane when it started to splutter and slid to a halt at the side of the road and conked out - no fuel left. I called at a nearby house and as I was ringing the doorbell I collapsed in a heap, hearing voices say "come in, come in, for heavens sake".

I next remember waking up in a warm bed with a kindly face looking down on me saying, "You had no business being out on a night like that".

My visitors book still has a full page devoted to the five amazing ladies who all signed as Mary and who would surely have perished had I not come along.

The Ripperage
A modern day Mary

We were invited for lunch at the Ripperage Inn by Andrew Machin, the man who showed me the famous order book dated 11 June 1906, which played such a part in unravelling the secret of Lily Cove in my book. Prior to lunch we signed some share certificates, as one of the long-term employees was becoming a director and shareholder in the company.

Our table was only booked for two p.m. because they were very busy. We arrived a little early to try and find a suitable table at which to sit. That proved to be a bit of a struggle but eventually we got a place and I produced the share certificate book and the members register going back many years. It was a rather formal but very pleasant experience and when it came time for Andrew and David to sign and seal the certificates I suggested that his two young sons should be the ones to operate the company seal as required in the Company's Memorandum and Articles of Association.

This all took place just before we were ready to go through for lunch.

Then I saw a really tall girl standing in the doorway to the kitchen in the statutory long black skirt and white top looking every inch the part of the extra waitress for the Xmas rush. She was exceptionally tall with jet-black hair on top with highlights or jewellery in her hair that added to its natural lustre. She had a long sharp but attractive nose and a very graceful neck and she was most attractive without being stunning. What drew me immediately to her was her height and a remarkable and striking resemblance to my heroine Mary Queen of Scots. As a bonus she filled her skirt well with a long slim pair of legs and pert bottom.

I knew I had to play this very carefully and so I went out to the car ostensibly to change into a more casual jersey and brought back with me a couple of the ghost books. Sitting next door to my wife I asked her in a fairly loud voice whether she noticed anyone in the room looking like Mary Queen of Scots. She was bound to look at the painting of her shown as an illustration in my book.

The likeness was stunning and she said so and I confirmed this with Andrew and Jane before calling across to the girl when she was serving the next door table. I told her that she had an amazing resemblance to Mary Queen of Scots although her eyes were even nicer than hers, if that was possible.
She seemed surprised but pleased and flattered at the same time.
Fortunately I had done it in such a way as not to frighten her and as I had told

her in front of the whole party everything was above board   Later as we were leaving I caught her and gave her one of my books as she told me her name was Amy and I put that with the inscription and my telephone number asking her to phone me once she had read the book.

I hope that she will be the next piece in the Lily Cove / Machin jigsaw puzzle - also because she is a cracker and it would be a joy to take her up to Sheffield with me to meet Mary.

I had hoped to talk to her before I went up to Sheffield Manor and rang Chris the owner of the Ripperage before I went.   Unfortunately she was not to be on duty on Christmas Day and so it was unlikely I would see her before the New Year.

I asked him to phone her to ask her to phone me but nothing has yet transpired.

All I wanted to do over Xmas was finish this book and now we have run out of kerosene fuel and it is damp and cold - wonderful! So there was no alternative but to go into town and buy a couple of heaters to keep off the chill until Brian McLuskie's man from Accent Fuels delivers new kerosene on Wednesday. So I went into town reluctantly thoroughly brassed off if the truth be told.

I went first to the Do it All store under the viaduct and found they had no heaters there. I said to myself must try every angle, follow every lead, so when I saw an amazingly tall chap with rather a long sharp nose, I asked him if he had a sister who worked at the Ripperage - No!

Off into Texas Do It Yourself, then I went to Curry's and they had quite good heaters and I asked them to hold a couple for me.

Then I went to see Terry at Intouch and had to wait a fair time to fix his payroll programme and then take a copy of Sargon3 the Chess Programme I had given to them probably eight years earlier.   It is only with some difficulty that I managed to copy it going back to basic MSDOS to do so.

I came out and walked quickly down towards Curry's and there she was striding across towards the Swan Centre!!   Amy!!   I caught up with her quickly and she seemed very pleased to see me.

Absolutely amazing coincidence - millions to one against our meeting especially as I was looking in Stourport and she lives in Cookley.

She is much taller than I thought - a full head higher than me - lovely eyes and soft mouth. She is 20 years old and lives with her boyfriend in Stourport.

I wished her a Happy Xmas, and said I would write with more photographs and pictures of Mary Queen of Scots. Unfortunately she is very thin and a fattening up programme will have to be undertaken!!

She had not yet started the book nor had the man from the Ripperage bothered to phone her. She promised to ring me after she has read the book. I also explained about my special relationship with Mary and how it would be a very friendly gesture to Mary to have Amy dress up like her to make her feel at home.

Wonderful turn round - I await the next meeting with interest and eager anticipation.

Unfortunately I now realise that Amy was just like the Mary everybody expected and depicted in all the portraits of her. You will however read later of how I have found someone who looks exactly like the real Mary – the one I have seen so many times – and how truly beautiful she is.

Floating Away
It is easy if you try

Every morning I fly with Mary Queen of Scots to one of four places:-

The Château de Guise
Babington Farm
Nether Kinnedar
Buxton Spa

All four are exciting and I leave the choice to her.

The Château de Guise
When we are content and merely wish to enjoy ourselves we travel back to France to happy times in warm sunshine and luxurious comfort at the Château de Guise.

Babington Farm
When we feel in need of home comforts we travel to Babington Farm my old country farmhouse where my Uncle Barnabas will welcome us saying, "Aunt Nellie is cooking up a lunch such you will never forget".

Nether Kinnedar
When we are cold we yearn for the front room at Nether Kinnedar where the fire will be roaring and the welcome as warm as the whisky and we know we are secure.

Buxton Spa
If our bones are aching and we don't feel one hundred percent then we head off to Buxton to the Spa where Mary has been so many times before. To take the waters to bathe in the 86 degrees warm natural Buxton water which has alleviated the aches and pains and sufferings of so many people.

You can come with us if you wish and you try hard enough. Imagine if you will lying in bed an hour before the alarm is due to go off. There's enough time if you have the will and the imagination.

Make sure first you are warm and the bedclothes have you fully covered. Drive your back gently into the warmth of the mattress beneath you and imagine your travelling companion in the crook of your right arm. Better still of course if your companion is really there beside you, but it matters not so long as your will is strong.

Sink deeper into the warmth beneath you, till your feet begin to rise and you can push yourself forwards and upwards with the palms of your hands. It is easy as pie if you try, and as you go, gather yourself together and imagine the place you are headed for.

Today, lets go to Buxton. Let's arrive in style on the Buxton Orient Express with luxurious coaches that cater for every comfort.
Get to your feet and feel the depth of the carpet and wiggle your toes so that they can feel the softness and warmth.

Then walk towards the attendant who has a huge towelling robe ready to enfold you in wool so soft it is like a second skin. Blue royal blue for men. Cerise royal cerise for the ladies the most flattering of colours.

Slip into the sandals placed just beside your toes and, glide gently towards the reception area where some warm mulled wine is ready for you.

In seconds you are transported into the luxurious world of the Buxton Spa where you will reinvigorate every part of your body and be pampered by experts in every field from Aromatherapy to mud baths.

Notice on your left lapel your adopted name of Charles - your name for the next three days and notice too that there beside you the elegant and exquisite Mary Queen of Scots.

She is tall and slim always seeming to tower above other mortals accentuated by her regal head-dress shaped in a heart shaped fan which shows her exquisite face and neck to perfection. What is it about this wonderful woman that makes all men fall in love with her and want to serve her, and all women seem to be in tune with her.

Before the second cup of mulled wine can be poured we are ushered into the corridor and as if by magic the ground seems to move and we are transported the short distance to the heart of the Spa.

"This way if you please" and there we sense for the first time the ambient humidity which is to be with us for all our stay. The pores on our skin can breathe and be cleansed and our bodies wish to be totally immersed in this lovely liquid which is clear as crystal and warm as toast and which clings to our skins in a silky way.

As we enter the water, strong hands relieve us of the gowns and we glide into the refreshing water never wishing to be dry again.

As you relax there, the alarm goes off and we are back in bed at home refreshed but determined to go on for longer tomorrow.

What will tomorrow bring?

The next day you learn to skip the first bit and zoom straight to the water and go on from there.   Frustratingly you are often held up by some irritating person keen to linger over the preliminaries and hold you back but you must be patient and each day go a little further.   Go to bed a little earlier and give yourself another ten minutes in the morning to explore those bathes.

I find that the warmth of the water comes more quickly and you have time to discuss with the pool side attendants what you will do when you finish your forty minutes in the pool.
You will learn that there are two men's pools called the two shilling pool and the one shilling pool and as much you think you can afford the two shilling pool maybe you haven't reached the point of deserving it. Both pools are the same temperature but the water comes from the natural spring and goes to the two shilling pool first and only then to the one shilling.

The Ladies Pool is exquisitely finished in wall tiles from floor to ceiling.
The floor is made of solid marble smoothed to perfection and showing all the natural colours of the rainbow. The ceiling is made of glass so that you can see the sun and the sky and the light glints on the waters of the pool.
The sides are tiled with a mosaic design so subtlety that the pool side attendants are camouflaged and with the expanse of colour that they fade into the background.

Mary Queen of Scots holds Court in the Ladies Pool and sits on a shelf specially designed for her so that only her head and shoulders emerge, keeping her hair and head-dress clear of the water.

Her subjects can approach her and converse with her, but they are a little surprised to hear her speak in French which has always been her favourite tongue since she went to France as a five year old and became the Queen of France.
She speaks so eloquently and so expressively that she appears to sing or chant and her words are remembered automatically as verses of a poem.

"What would you like to do to day today sir?" I am asked.

The author in the abandoned Ladies Pool before renovation

"A mud bath I think is called for, to eak out some of the excesses of the week and then a strong cold shower before lunch", and just as the man moves forward to help you from the pool, that blessed alarm goes off again.

"Surely I can hold it for longer" you tell yourself.

Mud is great fun. Warm sticky oozing mud made from the peat that has been formed from the succession of layers of deposit built up under pressure from the peat bogs of the dales. This is dug block by block cut by sharp spades and carried on carts back to the Spa.

Mixed with the warm water of the Spa, in tubs made of wood rather like barrels which are bound together with steel straps, to form a marvellous bath into which you are lowered till the mud squirms up past your body to reach the top of the bath level. If your attendants have judged the precise size of your body then not an ounce will be wasted by overflowing unnecessarily over the edge of the tub.

The feeling is one of intense intrusion into every part of your body from toe to tonsils from liver to bowel and everything but everything is first of all enveloped and compressed and then let free to exude all clean and fresh and bright and smelling so pure and natural that all blemishes are gone and every pore is clean.

It is mandatory that you insist that your partner also has a mud bath, because otherwise you could not be clean enough to be together.

The first drink you have after the mud bath, you fear will cascade through you and land on the floor as if every part of your body is open, and it is with amazement that you realise that are still self contained, and robust as well as being clean, and you can carry on with your life.

"Time sir for lunch and rejoining the ladies", and as you first notice the fragrance of the aromas of food, that darn alarm goes off once more.
What an appetite you have built up over the period as you are ravenous in the extreme.
Lunch is made up of sixteen dishes, each only a morsel it seems, but exquisite and subtle tastes. There is no choice and each one you must try with the knowledge that there is not a second mouthful but only the memory of that taste and the hope that tomorrow you will taste again that wonderful flavour.

The sixteen courses are taken at random - never in the same order - and that makes the pleasure of eating more exciting as the variations are endless.

Tiny pieces of venison in a gravy so rich and natural.

Courgettes so lightly boiled they are almost raw covered with a tiny sprinkling of sea salt.

Garlic beans like chickpeas only maybe twenty together in a squashed handful.

Chicken minced and fluffed with pastry so light it is hardly possible to weigh.

Red peppers so sweet and filled with cream.

The list is endless and the choice is never yours, but after sixteen your appetite is satisfied totally satisfied.

Your every action or reaction to each taste is registered by your attendant, so that at the next meal your favourites are somehow to the fore, or is that your imagination again as every course is exquisite.

Sleep is all now that you require, sleep and more sleep as those gastric juices overwhelm your conscious into a wonderful sleep.

When the alarm goes it is a monumental struggle to get up to the surface and wake up but you manage it screaming "surely it is not time yet".

Next morning when your slip away to the Spa you are waking from your post prandial nap and ready for the afternoon activities.

Who will your partner be for the afternoon game of cards and what game will you play? How is your bridge? Which conventions do you play? Or are you merely a gambler playing roulette?.

No - today we all play bridge with a partner selected by chance.

Sixteen players each draw a card from the pack and you pair off card by card. I drew a queen – could it be that my partner would be a queen also? Yes, of course, none other than my Queen of Scots who is a wonderful judge of cards. We make a great partnership because my mathematical mind can recall all the cards played and can judge the chances of each card being in the other players hand.

Bridge is a pleasure to play under whatever circumstance, but playing in the luxurious surroundings of the Buxton Assembly Rooms with each player seated in a perfectly fitting chair with your back at the right angle and your arms supported for minimum effort.

The square tables have green baize so that the cards slide effortlessly across to your partner or opponent and outside each arm lies a space perfectly placed to hold the crystal glass provided for you. Light sweet and cool with mint julep or the equivalent – no alcohol to fuzz the mind.

My Mary opens with one no trump and I have fourteen points and a singleton - a slam is possible - so I jump to three clubs. My partner responds with three diamonds and my long suit is diamonds. Can this be the perfect fit?
Four no trump I reply, asking for Aces and my Mary responds five spades showing all four! - What a partner.
As I also have one Ace this bid must mean that my partner has 3 Aces and a void suit. There can be no doubt now and "seven diamonds" is my bid.
"Double" cry our opponents but my Queen is not flustered and redoubles for maximum points.

I sit back and watch my wonderful partner scoop all thirteen tricks, trumping our only losing heart for a maximum result. No one else had the courage to bid seven diamonds and so we top the poll for the afternoon's play.

What a partner. And of course the rule is winning partnerships are kept to play again tomorrow. What joy that is, to know I will see my Queen again tomorrow.

"We must dress for dinner Sir" says my attendant just as the alarm goes off again

The tables are set out as they were in mediaeval times with a top table and then a long table at right angles so that no one has their back to anyone else.

Good for safety and reassurance that no one could stab you in the back!

A formal dinner with servants arriving with cauldrons of red hot soup made of vegetables and herbs and spices hot enough to warm you and fill you.
At the head table the centre is filled with a throne for Mary Queen of Scots and she is in residence tonight as we all defer towards her before tackling our starter.

"Will young Anthony please say grace!", commands Her Majesty and I rise to recite:-

>Some hae meat they canna eat
>Some lack meat that want it
>But we hae meat and we can eat
>So say the lord be thankit

The famous Selkirk grace penned by Robert Burns comes easily to mind.

The main course is salmon, a whole salmon, cooked to perfection and served whole for each person to slide off the bone just enough to satisfy their appetite without indulging in any greed.

Roast beef on the bone carved at the table by servants with white gloves. A rich gravy and roast potatoes with courgettes accompanies the roast.

To finish little mounds of chocolate covered with cream, just a touch for a taste of sweetness and luxury.

Rich deep coffee, black and strong, with a sharp mint to clean the palate.

I rise to toast our Queen and thank her for hosting a fabulous meal and she responds by thanking us for attending and saying that we must taste a liqueur which she has found in France for her Scots blenders to exploit. The taste of Drambuie is out of this world.

Sleep deep sleep is the only way to end a day such as this, and we all repose back to a sixteen bed dormitory under the ornately painted gallery sleeping as they did four hundred years ago all together, no privacy but no intrusion, all sleeping round our Queen.

No alarm could rouse me from this slumber.

What did Mary Queen of Scots look like?
How can one describe real beauty?

All reports of Mary state how beautiful and graceful she was but none are in any way specific. None of the portraits in any way do her justice.

We know she was tall and slim and regal, but what were her features really like?   All the portraits which have survived show her with a long straight aristocratic nose which seems fair, with rather hooded eyes which when looking down on you which could be most attractive.   Her mouth was always shown as pinched and very small and this apparently was the fashionable mouth of those days, possibly because teeth weren't as well cared for in those days and onc did not smile with big gaps in your teeth! But Mary had good teeth and loved to smile.

I don't think Mary had a small mouth at all, she had a lovely warm mouth and a generous smile and remember I am one of the very few people who have actually seen her.   The model in Madame Tussauds in London is excellent in every respect other than her mouth, which needs to be warmer and curl up at the corners rather than down.

People assume because Mary had a life with so much misery that she would look miserable, and I think this is a major folly, because it was her cheerfulness and good humour that saw her through those dreadful years of captivity. On the contrary when she broke into a smile it light up the room.

She was tall, six feet tall which was very tall for her day, and she was taller than most men which gave her a good psychological advantage over others.
If you look at her beautiful death mask you will see what a warm mouth she had and such a strong jaw and cheek bones. How I wish she could open those eyes and show us all what they were really like.

Her eyes are a little soulful and look to have enormous depths of passion both of joy and suffering, and look slightly downwards like Dorothy Malone.

Of course French was her natural language and she spoke with that french flair that defies description. I think the Scots she spoke in later life would have the hint of a French accent. She was athletic of course and a very good rider which stood her in good stead on many occasions.

There are apparently moves afoot to make a feature film on the life of Mary Queen of Scots backed by Fountainbridge Films who are apparently sticklers for historical accuracy so I hope Rhonda Tollefson is going to ask my advice on who should play the part of Mary. As I am the only person who knows precisely what she looks like that would seem to me a very sensible thing to do. On our website at **www.jockndoris.co.uk** we have shown pictures of a very tall attractive Danish girl called Leise Riber who shows a remarkable resemblance to Mary Queen of Scots.

What now?

I find myself at an amazing crossroads where there are at least eight roads joining together.   These are the strands of the plan to re-open the famous Spa at Buxton where Mary spent so many happy hours.

I am a Chartered Accountant and have many friends and colleagues who are experts in their own particular fields. I have drawn up an audacious plan to make use of their talents to open the Spa at Buxton.

We shall form a company called Buxton Spa Baths Ltd and it will have a share capital of £1,000,000.   I announced this at a public meeting in Buxton and offered to the residents there a controlling interest (or 51%) in this company.   Every householder will be offered 100 shares as a minimum for which they will pay £100. They may take more up to 100 shares for each family member. Shares will be allocated strictly on a geographical basis. Those nearest the Spa will be first. Louise Potter the owner of the Old Hall Hotel is the closest and will be first in line!

I hope every householder in the whole of Buxton takes up the shares because it their Spa that their company plans to open. Each shareholder will be entitled to use the pools every day of the year at a price which will be fixed at each Annual General Meeting. This will always be an economic but advantageous price.

The spa will be run for the benefit of all of Buxton which of course will include those guests of the Old Hall Hotel who have enjoyed rights to bathe there for many a long year and I expect the shareholders to agree that they too should have a beneficial rate.

Once The Crescent next door is re-opened (when and if Monumental Trust get off their Monumental backsides) then they too will be able to use the Spa.

We will advertise on the World Wide Web at **www.buxtonspa.com** and I expect people to come from far and near to enjoy the waters and their health giving qualities.

We plan to restore the Spa to its original glory, realising of course when we do, that the beautiful tiles there (counted recently at over 200,000) are over a hundred years old. They like all good citizens show their age to a degree and so not every tile will be pristine white but every tile will be lovingly polished and replaced only if absolutely necessary.

We will do the Ladies Pool first knocking a door through from the Pauper's Pit which is part of the Old Hall Hotel.

We plan a trial for a month once the Ladies Pool is operational again and will encourage the first hundred shareholders and all the guests of the hotel to use the pool and let us know how they find it.
Everything from the temperature and the feel of the crystal clear water to the potted plants and the waitress service.

We plan to have the pool exactly as it was with certain features added now made possible by modern technology. A Jacuzzi will whirl in one corner and both Sauna and Steam rooms will also be available.
Later there will be four different mud baths to enjoy with a special composite ticket for those intrigued enough and courageous enough to buy one.

Therapy rooms will be sectioned off and Massage, Aromatherapy, Homeopathy and Reflexology only some of the therapies on call.

Based on this trial a decision will be taken as to whether we proceed or not.
Failure is not an option. However if the pool is not wanted by the people of Buxton then it would not be a good plan to spend shareholders money on something not to be a success.

I know the decision will be positive and the shareholders money well spent.
Profits will be made and either ploughed back into the Spa for more facilities or paid to shareholders as a dividend for their wisdom in investing in the Spa.

A host of details need to worked out and many Quangos persuaded that it is a good idea, and that some of the strictest most rigid rules must be slackened just a little to give us space to breathe.
When the great opening day arrives I expect Marry Queen of Scots will grace the Spa with her presence. She has always insisted, when we have met there before, that I bring some of her famous but unique heather perfume which she so enjoys.

Any of you who catch a hint of this subtle fragrance, will know that her Majesty must have been there, because she is the only one allowed to use it.

She is tall at six feet and so elegant and graceful that it easy to see how she wowed both aristocrats, foreign diplomats and her own subjects with equal ease. She always wears her royal head-dress which is cap of shining silk in a heart shape with pearls as edging, and those of you lucky enough to see her will have no difficulty at all in recognising her.
Just wait and see!

What a trip to Copenhagen
Finding how beautiful she is

I regularly get a copy of a splendid monthly magazine called Lingerie Buyer intended for all those in the Clothing and Retail Trade. In the copy promoting the recent Exhibition in Harrogate, I saw for the first time a picture of a girl who was modelling the Change in Scandinavia range of lingerie.

As soon as I saw her, the hairs on the back of my neck stood up with excitement. I said to myself, "There is Mary Queen of Scots exactly like the Mary I have seen so many times".
I was determined to find this tall attractive girl so that I could show everyone how truly beautiful Mary was.

My search started at the Exhibition where I walked casually on to the stand to inquire about bath robes for the Buxton Spa Baths project and I was very courteously shown all they had to offer.
I was also given a whole range of leaflets - all of which were of the same beautiful girl. "Where can I get in touch with the photographer who took these pictures?" I asked, and Patricia Eve the owner of the stand asked very reasonably, "Why do you want to do so?"
I explained with complete honestly, "She is the splitting image of Mary Queen of Scots, and I would like to meet her! She might be able to play the part of Mary in the new film planned for next year."

"You had better contact the owner of the company in Copenhagen," said her husband, and they showed me his telephone number on the leaflets.
One phone call to Denmark and I spoke to Claus Walther Jensen who was very helpful. "Her name is Leise Riber and you must speak to Nanna Berg who runs Booking House, the agency employing Leise here in Copenhagen."
I phoned Nanna, who was charming, and told me her fax number so that I could introduce myself. This I did and after several faxes and emails I spoke to the lovely Leise on the phone.
I offered to come across to Copenhagen to meet her and she seemed pleased and so I arranged there and then to go the following weekend.
"Where should I stay?", I asked.
"The best hotel is the Hotel D'Angleterre and it is only one minute from our office!", said Nanna.
"Perfect", I said, "We will meet there on the Saturday afternoon.", and I booked a splendid room overlooking the Square. As I was keen to have photographs of the whole trip, I asked my friend John Pitt to join me. He always takes

excellent photographs of any subject you give him, and he became as excited as I was, to meet Leise.

Some time earlier, I had asked Sue Penzer the owner of Masquerade who make period costume for hire in Quinton, to make me a special head-dress for Mary to wear.

I wanted it to be exactly as I remember Mary wearing it, and I went to great lengths to design the high pieces above the head in a double crescent to highlight Her Majesty's beautiful eyes.

As it evolved we realised that those pieces must made of soft silk, and be near vertical so that Mary's hair could be set on top of her head and fill these areas. Eventually Janet, the wonderfully patient Janet, managed to make the Cap to my satisfaction and I knew instinctively that it would suit Leise Riber perfectly. We asked young Sarah to model it for us and she warmed to the part, also wearing Mary's black dress for us.

We chose period costumes from the Masquerade range, and I felt particularly comfortable in an outfit with amazing shoulders in gold braid and velvet trousers and white hose. Buckles for our shoes and we were ready to go.

John and I set off for Copenhagen from Birmingham Airport in buoyant mood, keeping however in mind my brother's favourite saying, "Blessed is he who expects nothing for he shall never be disappointed!"

A taxi swept us to the magnificent Hotel D'Angleterre where our room was next door to the Danny Kaye suite and overlooked the main Square in Copenhagen. We just had enough time to freshen up before our meeting with Leise.

Bang on time she walked majestically in to the reception area, and my breath was taken away by her height, her beauty and with the elegance and confidence she exuded. We almost stood on one another's toes, but neither of us minded, as I went forward to kiss her cheek which not surprisingly required to be made at full stretch. We invited her to join us at the table where we ordered tea and mineral water and started chatting as if we had known one another all our lives. She speaks beautiful English without a trace of accent and is fully as beautiful as I had hoped.

She had more of a tan than I had expected, but of course she is forever on modelling assignments in the sun, requiring her to look her best.

I explained at great length of my interest in Mary Queen of Scots and my meeting her as a ghost on several occasions. She was not phased by this at all, but took it all in her stride listening intently.

We went for a lovely walk all the way along the waterside cafes for which Copenhagen is famous. Everywhere eyes were turned towards us making me feel very proud to escort such a fabulous girl.

Later Nanna arrived and after the usual introductions we went upstairs to our room to show Leise the head-dress I had brought for her. As soon as she put it on, her eyes lit up with pleasure and it not only fitted her perfectly but also sent a shiver down my spine, as she looked exactly like Mary Queen of Scots standing there in our room.

She was obviously delighted with the Cap and was enthusiastic about wearing the dress again the next morning, when we planned a trip to Dragsholm Slot where Lord Bothwell had been imprisoned so cruelly four hundred years ago.

We all had a delightful dinner at the hotel sitting by the window almost in the Square with others walking past just feet away. We agreed to meet again the following morning at 9.45 and John and I had a large Drambuie to ensure we slept well.

John witnessed one of my famous mid-night jumps where for reasons unknown, I leap from the mattress, turn 90 degrees and land again still fast asleep. I have seen my younger son perform the same trick many times during his childhood, and only because of this, do I believe others who tell me that I do it.

The phone rang sharply at 8am, terrifying both of us and I answered the phone saying "Copenhagen here!" which at least showed I had remembered where we were.

I told John that I wanted to float away for ten minutes. I led him through my routine of driving my back into the mattress and with hands by my sides, push myself metaphorically into space, travelling effortlessly to the Chateau Guise in France where I had spent so much time with Mary Queen of Scots.

I described to John the scene and the climbing peach trees and plum trees rich with fruit, and he told me he could also see apricots, which took some doing!. Mary took me to one side and told me to stand tall and give her fondest wishes to Lord Bothwell, when we would see him later in the day.

We had a great breakfast, about four courses as I recall, and then went upstairs to change into our costumes for the day. John and Nanna thought they might steal our thunder so they decided to stay in modern dress, whilst Leise and I turned a few heads on the grand staircase as we descended to the foyer.

We climbed into Nanna's trusted Audi and she drove effortlessly (and with only one detour caused by a back seat driver!) to Dragsholm Slot. There to meet us in a majestic red dress and white powder wig was Nina our guide who started to show us round the castle. She was enthusiastic and spoke perfect English but all I wanted to do was to explore quietly, without the distraction of any narrative.

I asked Nina to show us where the dungeon was, and I formally escorted Leise as Mary Queen of Scots by the arm. As we took the stairs down to the lowest part of the building, the transformation into Mary Queen of Scots was complete. I found a chair for Her Majesty to sit on, which had so much dust on it, it could well have been four hundred years old.

There I was surprised to see two effigies - one clearly Lord Bothwell sitting forlornly at a table with one arm heavily bandaged, as he had gangrene which was eventually to kill him.
On the floor lay another prostrate figure on a bed made out of just a little straw and a thin blanket.
I was told this was John Clark, who had been sent by the Scots Lords to spy on Bothwell, and who stayed almost four years for his trouble in the most unspeakable misery, without getting any information from Lord Bothwell.

I stood with Mary as we both looked at John Clark who's eyes blazed and I felt the most appalling hate towards this man, with almost a physical loathing which frightened me.

Bothwell looked towards us and said , " Don't worry - I will strangle him with my bare hands before I die. I could not bear to be entombed with him any longer. It will not be the first man I have strangled - as that rogue Darnley required the same fate. I need no longer deny that I killed him, for everyone knows my dear Queen had nothing whatever to do with it."

"What news from my wonderful Queen?," he asked. I replied that she sent her fondest greetings but there was no way she could come to visit him herself. "We must stand tall", she said. She was immeasurably proud of Bothwell who had endured so much in this dreadful prison.
"I want to be laid to rest with my mistress and Queen," said Bothwell. "Please take my head (for my body is long since scattered by my jailers) to rest beside my Queen at Chatsworth.
"But is not Her Majesty to be found at Westminster Abbey?" I exclaimed.
"No - they want you to think that, but secretly the Earl of Shrewsbury had her body removed from Peterborough to Chatsworth for safety and no one has ever found out!", said Lord Bothwell. "You will find her in Queen Mary's Bower at Chatsworth and that is where I would like to take my rest."
"This lovely lady bears a remarkable resemblance to my beloved Mary," Bothwell continued, "but no one could ever match her beauty - tell the world how beautiful she was and that she was not implicated in Darnley's death. I strangled him because he deserved nothing less - he never showed any respect for Her Majesty. I shall rest easy now knowing that I will soon be at peace with

my Queen again. Thank you for travelling to see me and make sure you tell my story the way it was.", said Lord Bothwell.

With that the lovely girl beside me started showing signs of distress, and we very shakily ascended the stairs where the rest of the party were seated. We sat for some while trying to get back to normality but the experience had drained us of energy.

Later we went and explored the rest of this amazing castle which had at least six or seven ghosts, and a very marked fault across an area now used as a Theatre. This prevented John's camera from working when he stood in the fault line.

Leise warmed into the role of Mary and as John looked for locations to take photographs, several stunning shots were taken which are found later in this book. Leise is the ideal Mary and I hope she is asked to play the part in the forthcoming film, because she matches almost perfectly the wistful beauty of Mary Queen of Scots and we have a duty to show everyone how attractive and beautiful Mary was.

We drove back to Copenhagen in a state of excitement only stopping for a wonderful frankfurter sausage for lunch with Leise and Nanna demonstrating wonderful appetites at a Stef Houlberg stand where we almost ate them out of a month's supply of sausages.

John and I bade a fond farewell to our wonderful hosts and headed for the airport and home. I slept throughout the flight and all the way through till late the next morning we were so exhausted by the exhilarating experiences.

Not till Thursday did we see the photographs which were excellent and which now are on the web site at **www.leise-riber.com** for all to see. I know when Rhonda Tollefson sees these, she will have no alternative but to look most closely at Leise Riber for the part of Mary. I am also told by an impeccable source, that there is strong possibility that the part of Anthony Babington will go to a Chartered Accountant in a gold doublet and velvet trousers, although who that could be, I know not!

THE BEAUTIFUL MARY QUEEN OF SCOTS
Some haunting pictures of Leise Riber as Mary Queen of Scots:-

All the pictures in this book have been taken by John Pitt, Photographer of Abberley, Worcs WR6 6AY. Those that follow show the lovely girl found in the last chapter, who matches almost perfectly the wistful beauty of Mary Queen of Scots seen so often by the author.

For years the author has been frustrated at not being able to show to the world how truly beautiful Mary Queen of Scots was. Now through Leise Riber, the attractive young model from Copenhagen, he has captured her beauty and elegance and authority on the following pages.

Readers who believe Mary Queen of Scots never smiled, should proceed no further and return the book to the bookshelf. But then they would miss that devastating smile and those sparkling eyes that have captivated every man and woman and child fortunate enough to see them.

There are more pictures on our Websites
at **www.jockndoris.co.uk** and **www.leise-riber.com**

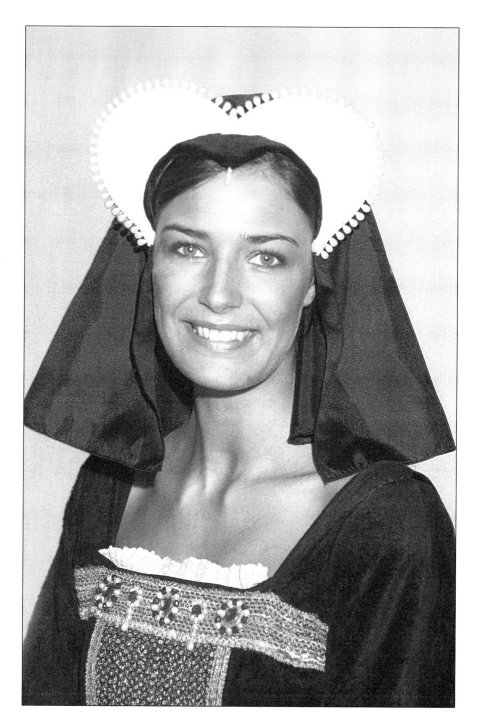